1,000,000 Books

are available to read at

Forgotten Books

www.ForgottenBooks.com

Read online
Download PDF
Purchase in print

ISBN 978-1-331-62184-3
PIBN 10214177

This book is a reproduction of an important historical work. Forgotten Books uses state-of-the-art technology to digitally reconstruct the work, preserving the original format whilst repairing imperfections present in the aged copy. In rare cases, an imperfection in the original, such as a blemish or missing page, may be replicated in our edition. We do, however, repair the vast majority of imperfections successfully; any imperfections that remain are intentionally left to preserve the state of such historical works.

Forgotten Books is a registered trademark of FB &c Ltd.
Copyright © 2018 FB &c Ltd.
FB &c Ltd, Dalton House, 60 Windsor Avenue, London, SW19 2RR.
Company number 08720141. Registered in England and Wales.

For support please visit www.forgottenbooks.com

1 MONTH OF FREE READING

at

www.ForgottenBooks.com

By purchasing this book you are eligible for one month membership to ForgottenBooks.com, giving you unlimited access to our entire collection of over 1,000,000 titles via our web site and mobile apps.

To claim your free month visit:

www.forgottenbooks.com/free214177

* Offer is valid for 45 days from date of purchase. Terms and conditions apply.

English
Français
Deutsche
Italiano
Español
Português

www.forgottenbooks.com

Mythology Photography **Fiction** Fishing Christianity **Art** Cooking Essays Buddhism Freemasonry Medicine **Biology** Music **Ancient Egypt** Evolution Carpentry Physics Dance Geology **Mathematics** Fitness Shakespeare **Folklore** Yoga Marketing **Confidence** Immortality Biographies Poetry **Psychology** Witchcraft Electronics Chemistry History **Law** Accounting **Philosophy** Anthropology Alchemy Drama Quantum Mechanics Atheism Sexual Health **Ancient History** **Entrepreneurship** Languages Sport Paleontology Needlework Islam **Metaphysics** Investment Archaeology Parenting Statistics Criminology **Motivational**

UNIV. OF
CALIFORNIA

N. BOOTH TARKINGTON, 1917

BOOTH TARKINGTON

BY
ROBERT CORTES HOLLIDAY

Illustrated

GARDEN CITY   NEW YORK
DOUBLEDAY, PAGE & COMPANY
1918

Copyright, 1918, by
DOUBLEDAY, PAGE & COMPANY

*All rights reserved, including that of
translation into foreign languages,
including the Scandinavian*

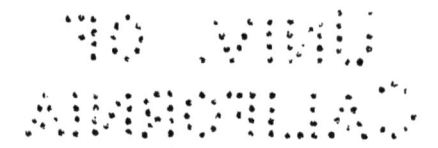

TO
B. T.

392440

ACKNOWLEDGMENT

Curiously enough, just about the time that Mr. Tarkington began to be of serious critical interest practitioners of literary criticism beyond the compass of a "review" of one book left off with him. Thus this little study is able to arrive at ultimate conclusions quite different from any estimate of Mr. Tarkington that I have ever seen in print. I have, however, in the course of my thought drawn very liberally upon a number of "sources." Where I have been in accord with the opinion of writers of earlier, much briefer, studies, I have not hesitated to adapt their ideas to my purpose. I am beholden in particular, for information, suggestions, and stimulation, to the following excellent books and articles:

"Some American Story Tellers," by Frederick Taber Cooper; "The Advance of the English Novel," by William Lyon Phelps; "Representative American Story Tellers: Booth Tarkington," by Arthur Bartlett Maurice, in the *Bookman*, February, 1907; "The Hoosiers," by Meredith Nicholson; "John-a-Dreams," Personal and Critical Sketch, *Pearson's Magazine*, March, 1903; "The Development of the English Novel" (though it has nothing about Mr. Tarkington in it), by Wilbur Cross; the little magazine *John-a-Dreams*; an article by C. H. Garrett in the *Outlook*, 72:817; and personal sketches in *Current Literature*, 30:280; *Critic*, 36:399; *Harper's Weekly*, 46:1773.

For the record of my first view of Mr. Tarkington I have, by the courtesy of the Indianapolis *Star*, drawn upon an article of mine, "Impression of Literary Celebrities Gathered by a Returned Native," which appeared in that newspaper. The little story about Mr. Tarkington and the professor was one time contributed to the New York *Evening Post*.

R. C. H.

New York, December 15, 1917.

FOREWORD

What a joke it is now, that gay old affair, which was all about a few years ago, the gift book, stuffed full of straw and bound in tinsel. Happily it is as dead to-day as the horsehair sofa, the wax flowers of the old mantle, and bisque statuary. And its place has been taken by something not unworthy of the name of book.

It would be, as they say in England, "a jolly good job, too," if all our flood of "blurb" tales about living authors, as florid and as empty as the gift book, could go the way of that quaint memory. In other countries, indeed, there is nothing new about the idea of considering a literary figure of the day with an effort at honesty and intelligence. In England it seems to be quite the fashion to get up all the while very respectable little biographical and critical affairs about Mr. Wells and Mr. Chesterton, Mr. Shaw and Mr. Galsworthy. And we do have knocking about over here admirable little books about foreign writers such as Conrad, Anatole France, and the one-time American Mr. James. But certainly we have rather neglected to pry into living home talent.

Nothing, however, is now as it was. Everyone wants to know more about the value of what one is doing than one did before the war. And decided indeed has been the effect of this general quickened mental alertness upon reading. Books are more carefully chosen; much more is demanded of them.

And that is the excuse for this somewhat novel proceeding: a little book (which, with all its multiplicity of failings, fears bunkum like the devil) about a gentleman who certainly must be held a thoroughly characteristic American writer. Mr. Tarkington, as one of our most popular novelists, should be a thoroughly legitimate object of attack. Has he got any justification for being around these days and for going on? Are you making a decent use of your time in reading him? Ought all his early books to be scrapped? And how, exactly, did he come about, anyhow?

There is, I think, more or less to be said about that.

LIST OF ILLUSTRATIONS

N. Booth Tarkington, 1917.................*Frontispiece*
Mr. Tarkington's Study at Kennebunkport,
    Maine...........................*Facing Page 198*

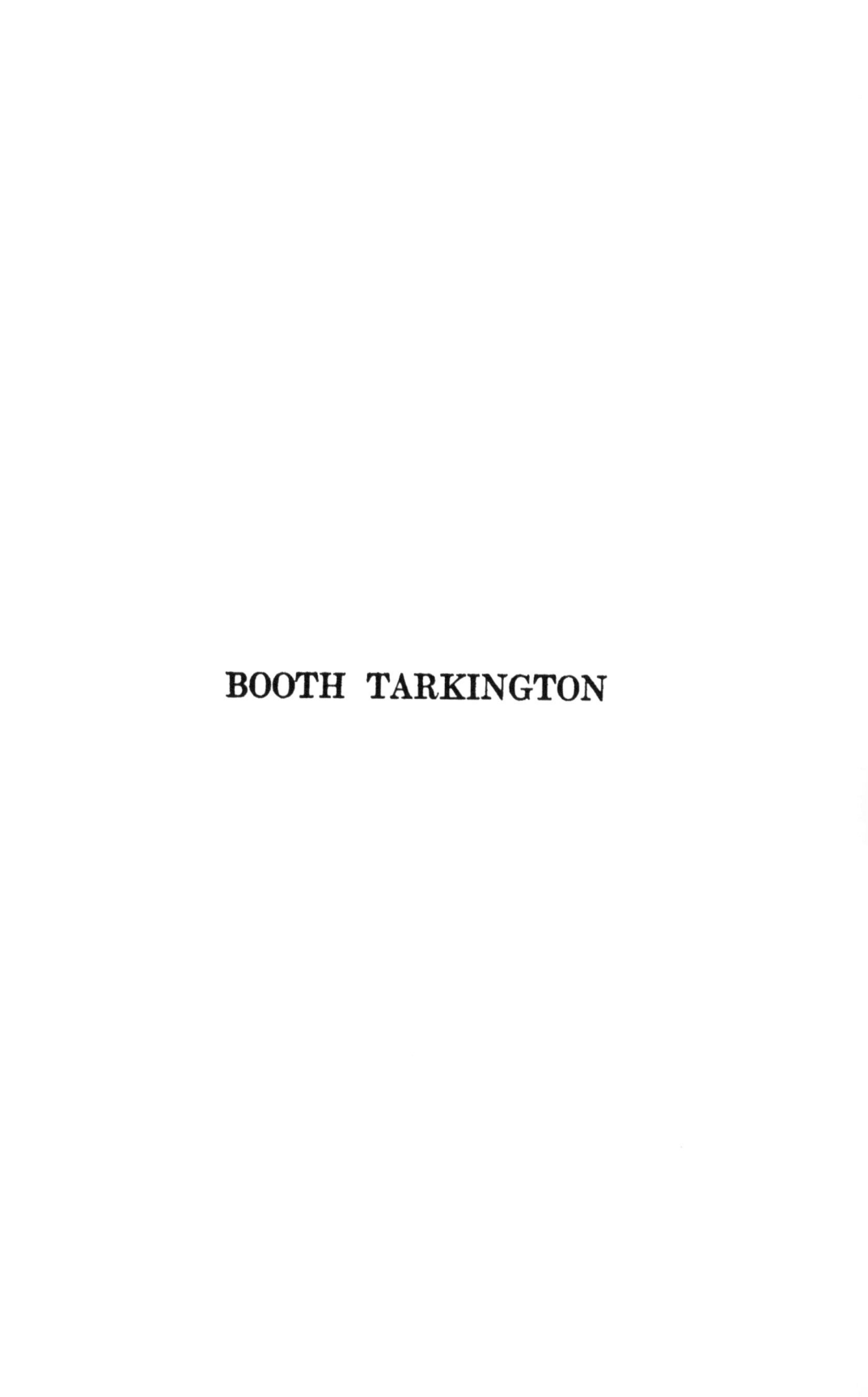

BOOTH TARKINGTON

I

IN contemplating the idea of Mr. Tarkington one is struck at the outset by an arresting reflection. It is impossible to avoid the assumption that, whether or not he has "made good," the gods had something decidedly unusual in mind in the matter of his existence.

Anyone who has considered, ever so lightly, the springs of English literature has been amazed by the frequency of the presence, well-nigh inevitable in the background, of the minister who was father, or at least grandfather, to the writer. It would seem that whenever Nature had a man of letters up her sleeve the first gift with which she has felt it necessary to dower him has been a preacher sire. It has also, everybody knows, been the rule that men of brilliant minds have had mothers of intellectual tastes—though sometimes the fathers seem to have been negligible. Further, there is something fascinating to the inquiring mind, and doubtless of psychological significance, in the fact of so many celebrated writers having at first mistakenly felt their vocation to be that of the "artist," as the term is popularly understood. Hazlitt, for instance, and George Moore, and the author of *The Way of All*

Flesh, and a lot more, all went at the world in the belief that they were called to interpret it in the medium of paint. The most illustrious instance of the frustrated ambition to be an illustrator of other men's books is, of course, Thackeray. But there is almost no end to the cases in which a desire to draw is found to have been lurking in an author's past. Robert W. Chambers first intended to be an illustrator. O. Henry had an itch for making pictures before he found himself. And the spirited illustrations Gilbert Chesterton has made for the books of his friend Mr. Belloc leave no doubt that he would have been as much of an *enfant terrible* as an illustrator as he is a journalist.

So, it surely was "up to" Mr. Tarkington to (as the title of a British painting of some years ago which I recall has it) "for God's sake do something or be something!" If, on the strength of having been born with a silver spoon in his mouth, he had "lain down" altogether he certainly would have flouted a singular beneficence of the fates. All the auspicious morning stars sang together at his birth. His paternal grandfather was a pioneer minister of Indiana; one of his grandmothers wrote poetry; his mother was distinguished in the community of her residence for her intellectual character, and organized the first woman's club in a locality where there are now perhaps more women's clubs in proportion to population than in any other place in the world; he early was inwardly impelled to make pictures; and he was born' in a spectacular "literary center" of the United States quite at the right moment to be in at the hour of its bursting into literary flower.

While it is undoubtedly true that we know very little about a talent till we know where it grew up, the general facts of Mr. Tarkington's "growing up" have already been so fairly well disseminated that to retell them here would, maybe, have the sound of "old stuff." Amid all our wealth of authors, few, if any, have provoked a more popular interest—a public interest peculiarly touched with a spirit of personal attachment—than the author of *Monsieur Beaucaire* and *The Gentleman from Indiana*. And the likeness of Mr. Tarkington's features, it may be said offhand, is probably as widely and as instantly recognized as that of George Washington or Colonel Roosevelt. Much water has flowed under the mill, however, since the newspapers and magazines vied with one another in heralding this "young writer," in news articles and personal sketches, as "an American of to-morrow." Mr. Tarkington has become, like the Statue of Liberty, an established fact among us, whose origin is now discussed only by foreigners. And, glancing back, there may be several new things to be said, and some things to be said to our purpose here about what has been said, and perhaps forgotten.

Mr. Tarkington was born in Indianapolis in 1869. He is a descendant of the Reverend Thomas Hooker, a noted scholar and orator of Revolutionary fame; his great-grandmother was Mary Newton, who figures as a beauty in the Annals of Old Salem. Mary Newton made a runaway match with a soldier of the Revolution, Walter Booth. It is not true, as has somewhere been said (though one feels that by rights it should have been so), that from these were descended the Booths who were the pride and glory of the American stage forty odd years ago. Another family altogether, that. Mary Newton's Walter Booth was not an actor, nor were any of his descendants of the "profession"; though the *instinct* of the actor, the mimic, one gathers from Mr. Tarkington, did repeatedly crop out in the blood of the Tarkington Booths. Mr. Tarkington's family have been prominent in Indiana for three generations He was named for his uncle Newton Booth, a native of Salem, Indiana,—the birthplace also of the author, diplomat, and cabinet officer, John Hay,—one time governor of California, senator from that State, prominent as an orator throughout his public career. In attempting to explain some of Mr. Tarkington's temperamental predilections, a purely imaginary Gallic strain in his ancestry has been invented, on his father's side of the house. His father, John Stevenson Tarkington, an Indiana lawyer and soldier of the Civil War, distinguished among his associates as a gentleman of the old school, and familiarly known as "Judge" Tarkington, partook in his prime of the meat and drink of all authentic Indianians, politics, and sat for a time in the State legislature; the leisure of his later years he has employed in literary work, and is the author of two books. His *Hermit of Capri*, published in 1910, reveals a pleasant fanciful vein that is quaintly individual. All of the novelist's family for several generations have had a bookman quality, though Mr. Tarkington, jealous of their good name, is very quick to insist that they have never been "offensively" book people. "At least," he says, "I don't *think* so."

Booth Tarkington himself, by all accounts, was very precocious up to about the age of four. He further fixed himself very beautifully in every tradition of persons destined to literary fame by being a "queer child." His oddities, one gathers, were even more odd than is usual with odd children. For one thing, he had a "Hunchberg family." Just so! Exactly such a "circle of friends," his "Invisibles," as that possessed by Hamilton Swift, Junior, queer "little father of dream children," celebrated, some thirty-five years later, in *Beasley's Christmas Party*. Whether "Mister" Tarkington had also a Simpledoria and a Bill Hammersley, I cannot say; but I think it highly probable. Indeed, I understand, there was just such a glorious make-believe party given for him as that staged by the Honorable David Beasley for his dismayingly active-minded little charge, "Mister Swift."

After about four, Mr. Tarkington says, he was "not precocious at all"; and he was, he affirms, "slow" at school; which condition in early education, by the way, is yet another peculiarity not infrequently remarked in children who later develop conspicuous mental powers. Mr. Tarkington becomes even preposterous in the lengths to which he went (unwittingly no doubt) to oblige the requirements, both sentimental and scientific, for every early symptom of latent genius. In his childhood he even suffered certain nervous disorders, "nearly St. Vitus" attacks; which have in some cases, according to learned men, borne a relation to the activities of brilliant minds. It is pleasanter, however, to turn from this rather recondite point to note an event, held in store by the beneficent destiny which selected his birthplace, which undoubtedly did much to set the tune of his mind. That was the beginning of his association with a figure about whom most of us can never hear too much, though this gentleman was not quite so much of a universal figure at that time. Mr. Tarkington began his friendship with Riley, a neighbor, when he was about eleven years old; and he acknowledges (shaking his head in reflection at the depth of it) that the spirit of Riley has exercised over him a strong, if often unconsciously felt, influence all his life.

If (as Mr. James declares) the first fact which goes a great way to explain the composition of Stevenson is that the boyhood of the author of *Kidnapped* was passed in the shadow of Edinburgh Castle, it is equally true that it would halt terribly at the start any account of the work of Mr. Tarkington which should omit to insist promptly that he grew up in the neighborly and cozy big country town (as it was then) of Indianapolis. Even now, "the man across the street or next door," says Mr. Nicholson in his essay "*A Provincial Capital,*" "will share any good thing he has with you, whether it be a cure for rheumatism, a new book, or the garden hose." And, "it is a town where doing as one likes is not a mere possibility, but an inherent right."

Much of the local color of Mr. Tarkington's boyhood in the middle-western town which was his home is of course reflected in the boy stories of his middle life. The topography of his youthful orbit, one perceives, comprised as its most salient features "alleys," stables, yards, fences, "cisterns," and porches, with more or less perfunctory rounds to Sunday School, dancing class, and "Ward School,

Nomber Seventh." He was a town boy; neither a city, nor a country, boy. The pleasant flavor of a thoroughly representative American town, which he imbibed in his early formative years, permeates nearly all his work; and it is his very honest feeling for the charm of just such a place that, one cannot fail to note, gives a strength to much of his rosy sentiment,—and, later, driving force to his satire. The precocious eccentricities of Mr. Tarkington's tenderest years did not interfere with his being a remarkably boy-like boy when the time came for that, so one gathers from his intimate knowledge of the hair-raising inner workings of the minds of Messrs. Penrod Schofield, Samuel Williams, and the rest of that now illustrious "limited bachelor set." In fact, the exuberance of spirits, spontaneity, and infectious joy of life which Mr. Tarkington exhibited in his 'teens linger among the traditions of the neighborhood of his boyhood. A tradition substantiated by Mr. Tarkington's confession that the Penrod stories cost him no effort, and involve **no** contemporary observation of boys—though boys, he says, are pretty near the most interesting things there are. The Penrod stories, in short, one feels may be taken to represent Mr. Tarkington's way of writing what Mr. James, in his title of an account of a very different boy, called *A Small Boy and Others.* Mr. James is more than discreet in this volume; he is reticence itself. Mr. Tarkington's every book is the soul of candor.

Seventeen, as the reviewers have noted, may be read as "a clever caricature, a 'rattling good story,' a 'gay analysis of calf-love,' a serious study in adolescent psychology, or a remarkable picture of small-town American life," that is, a truthful transcript of juvenile manners at the time of, so to put it, the author's "first-dress-suit period." Penrod was a novelist, and William Baxter a poet. And not only Mr. Tarkington's vivid presentation of their dissimilar inspirations, but the character of their literary productions, proclaims beyond doubt the autobiographic touch. In his abortive fragments of fiction, Penrod is a much better novelist (albeit a bit blood curdling) than "William Sylvanus Baxter, Esq." (as he signs himself), is a poet. And so, indeed, is the creator of both these writers. In fact, there is something decidedly prophetic about the turn of the embryonic talent of the youthful author of *Harold Ramorez*, with its unforgettable passages such as this:

The remainin scondrel had an ax which he came near our heros head with but missed him and remand stuck in the wall. Our heros amumition was exhaused what was he to do, the remanin scondrel would soon get his ax lose so our hero sprung forward and bit him till his teeth met in the flech for now our hero was fighting for his very life. At this the remanin scondrel also cursed and swore vile oaths.

For (one fancies) was not the boy author of *Harold Ramorez* father to a man also strongly drawn to depicting scenes of darkly romantic drama, and one who came to paint with gusto, and much ability, scenes of carnage? For one instance, the grim automobile accident, an uncommonly impressive bit of pictorial writing, in *The Guest of Quesney*.

Mr. Baxter's poems were of lovely ladies. And so were (those preserved to us in an early magazine) Mr. Tarkington's. Mr. Baxter excelled in sincerity when he wrote:

MILADY

I do not know her name
Though it would be the same
Where roses bloom at twilight
And the lark takes his flight
It would be the same anywhere
Where music sounds in air
I was never introduced to the lady
So I could not call her Lass or Sadie
So I will call her Milady
By the sands of the sea
She always will be
Just Milady to me.

Mr. Tarkington, having the advantage of a university education, excelled merely in artistry, when, sometime in 1896, he wrote:

THE PROUD LOVER

Nay, never wave your fan at ME
   To come, and kneel, and tie your shoe—
I'll stiffly seem most slow to see;
   Or, if I turn, will gaze at you
With coldness. High and haughtily
   I hold me, ma'am; I was not made
To bend me in servility;
   I'll bend—sometimes—to kiss your brow,
   But never low as shoe-lace bow!
—What ails the minx?—she's coming here,
   I will reprove her insolence;
My troth she has—but ne'er De Vere
   Brooked any such impertinence!
    .   .   .   .   .   .

   The other's loose, as well, you say?
—'T is tied. That's all, my love, to-day?

The sentiment, in both poems, is the same.

II

MR. TARKINGTON took to "college" as a duck to water. He took a spin at Phillips Exeter Academy to "prepare" for what was with him indeed a "college career." Mr. Tarkington's going to college may be fancifully compared in effect to Conrad's marriage with the sea. At Exeter Academy he began to open into flower. His pranks and exploits there (I have heard) are still recalled as among the brightest spots in the recollection of the distant youth of his classmates. And there the orator and writer in his blood began to "break out on him." He attracted besides some attention as the illustrator of the class yearbook. He went next to Purdue University, at Lafayette, Indiana, a sister institution to the Indiana State University; and here doubtless he got rubbed in another layer of the native Hoosier soil, which was later to be of such value in determining the temper of his work. Though "Purdue" is the State school of technology, it is not diligent in the sciences to the neglect of the arts. And Mr. Nicholson, in his little history, *The Hoosiers*, speaks of Lafayette as "one of the most attractive of Indiana cities, fortunate in its natural setting and in the friendliness of its people to all good endeavors."

An article signed "N. Booth Tarkington '93," which appeared in an old number of *The Nassau Literary Magazine*, begins: "Fifteen persons, who had once defined themselves simply—and completely —as Yale men, and one person for whose answers to inquiries about himself the word 'Princeton' (spoken in a tone of reserve) had sufficed, sat in the office room of the University Club." "Princeton man" (one may say) defined Mr. Tarkington, not simply, but eloquently, joyously, and completely, in (as the well-worn poetic phrase has it) the bloom of his young manhood. Probably nobody ever had a college career which has been so widely relished, so much celebrated and sung, as that of Mr. Tarkington's. And probably nobody can quite understand Mr. Tarkington's success as a novelist, or, altogether, his books themselves, without turning back for a peep at the gay spectacle of his Princeton days. He studied to some extent, no doubt, as, it is recorded, he stood well in his class, according to the curriculum. But that, one suspects, was merely an incident, resulting from the natural quickness of his mind. He is reported to have said that he has no doubt that he imbibed some education at Princeton; "though it seems to me that I *tried* to avoid *that* as much as possible."

A writer whose authority is evident in his signing himself "John-a-Dreams" (the name of an intimate magazine of a little clique with which Mr. Tarkington was associated directly after leaving college), writing in a magazine "appreciation" sometime after Mr. Tarkington "sprang" into national popularity, testifies that the college Tarkington was never a plodder. This writer, in *Pearson's Magazine*, says: "In fact, to see him walking across the campus with his sweater turned up about his neck and his hands thrust deep in his trousers' pockets, or to catch a glimpse of him hurrying nervously along in evening clothes, would readily give the impression that he never worked at all." And of this college "man," the writer adds that perhaps he felt intuitively that he did give this impression, for shortly after his first literary "success," in *naïve* seriousness, he explained to a classmate that he "really did a lot of hard work on the thing."

It is highly probable that Mr. Tarkington would have made a mess of it if routine labor had, unhappily, been his portion. I know a man who suffered a nervous breakdown from an office job of literary hack work to whom Mr. Tarkington said, "I couldn't have done it." He is of the highly-strung type, the fine temperament, capable of soaring flights (and in later years of demoniac energy), for whom the sustained effort commonly called work is made possible only by intense interest and enthusiasm in what it undertakes. Drudgery would probably have broken him; poverty have blighted him altogether. He is not of the stamp of those who have made two and two come five; who have toiled at hard labor, meaningless to them, in an engine room or at a desk, or have tended bar (as literary men have done), for eight to ten hours a day, and have welded literature in a long day of their own wrung from hours allotted by nature to sleep. One cannot make such a hero of this Harry Fielding. He was made for the sun; and the sun, nothing backward in its duty here, shone on him.

Professor Phelps, in his volume *The Advance of the English Novel*, has seen in *Bibbs* of *The Turmoil* a resemblance to the author. Professor Phelps' vision (it strikes one) is a peculiar one for anyone to have who has ever looked upon Mr. Tarkington. Though, at the most, this much is undoubtedly true: compulsory employment in a machine shop would probably have had about the same effect on Mr. Tarkington that it had on *Bibbs*. The graceful and unconscious ease of Mr. Tarkington's attitude toward life in his Princeton years was so irresistible that his classmates had their joke upon it, and applied to him the words of a popular Glee Club song he used to sing:

> I've been working on the railroad,
>   All the livelong day;
> I've been working on the railroad,
>   To pass the time away.

The undergraduate Mr. Tarkington had a kind of genius for American college life: he was, apparently, in everything and of everything that made for good fellowship. Such, it seems, were the qualities of his heart and mind made manifest there that he has become one of the bright legends of Princeton. His popularity there, both as an undergraduate and to this day, is notorious. Jesse Lynch Williams, and divers and sundry others of his classmates, have graved the eulogy again and again. No doubt he can never live it down: he was one of the young lions of his day, and as such has passed into a proverb.

Speak they, say they, tell they the Tale:

Mr. Tarkington entered his class at Princeton at the beginning of his junior year. During this year *The Tiger* (the college comic weekly) was revived; some say Mr. Tarkington revived it; at any rate, he was soon numbered among its editors, and his contributions, in text and pictures, to it for a long period probably were of considerable aid in giving it the important place it holds in college journalism. In collaboration with a fellow student Mr. Tarkington wrote an opera, which he staged and directed, taking at the same time an important part in the cast,—and as an actor was also very "popular." The play met with such response that it was given for three successive years. This genie of college life ate and smoked and gossiped with the Ivy Club; he (though Mr. Tarkington has never been personally active in outdoor games) sympathized with and loyally supported the athletic teams (and still usually gets to Princeton in the autumn at football time); he wrote the prize class song, and sang and travelled with the Glee Club, in which he was soloist, and for which he wrote many, or most, of its songs. Poe's *Raven* was one of the pieces that he set to music.

The "quiet playfulness" which "pervaded" (as Penrod says), "our hero," the Princeton "star"; his "delicious, unconscious drollery"; his "mobile, serio-comic facial expressions"; his wit, "ever brilliant, never boisterous"; his "saving sense of humor," which enabled him to appreciate keenly a joke on himself; these are things which have always been fondly emphasized by his college mates in their published "personal sketches." And this great "card" (in Mr. Bennett's term) was, by all accounts whatever, also a Sensitive Plant. He took, one hears, all the hubbub he stirred up, with the utmost good humor; and his shyness is as proverbial as his "greatness,"—and, naturally, must have had a good deal to do with it, as nothing (they say) is more captivating in a popular idol than a dash of the "modesty of the school-girl." There is, of course, the classic tribute to this young lion's doe-like nature. One of the little world of men who enjoyed him first has expressed his sentiment about him in some verses which hang on the walls of the Princeton Club of New York, beside an original sketch of an interesting-looking gentleman in evening clothes, who suggests James J. Corbett, but who is intended to represent Mr. Tarkington singing "Danny Deever." The verses, doubtless, you know:

Rondel

The same old Tark—just watch him shy
  Like hunted thing, and hide, if let,
  Away behind his cigarette,
When "Danny Deever!" is the cry.

Keep up the call and by and by
We'll make him sing, and find he's yet
    The same old Tark.

No "Author Leonid" we spy
  In him, no cultured ladies' pet:
  He just drops in, and so we get
The good old song, and gently guy
The same old Tark—just watch him shy!

In his circle Mr. Tarkington's singing of Kipling's ballad, "The Hanging of Danny Deever," seems to have been a whole lot like Edward FitzGerald's translation of the *Rubáiyát* of Omar Kháyyám. He sort of made the thing. He was apparently called upon to sing it upon every available occasion. The student of the life and "good times" of Mr. Tarkington is given, by Mr. "John-a-Dreams," a fragrant picture of young hearts: After dinner, in fine weather, before the steps of Old North College, where it is the privilege of the seniors to discourse college songs, Mr. Tarkington was, when he showed himself (it is told), invariably compelled to give his great hit.

There was no escape for him from the vociferous demand, except to slink away under cover of the gathering dusk; which he frequently did, from a feeling that too much prominence was being given to his performance as distinct from the general character of the singing. Though at first he would sit and plead with his companions to "go on and sing something else"; but latterly, realizing the futility of any appeal, he resorted to bodily escape as soon as the cry of "Tark! Tark! Danny Deever!" was raised.

And the same cry continued to be raised long after Mr. Tarkington's senior year wherever he joined himself to a quorum of his college mates; who called, exactly as they did years before, for exactly the same performance by which they measured his popularity then; and he yielded with the same nervous embarrassment as when he was first made to sing it.

This matter has here been belabored at such a great rate quite in the interest of literary criticism: in order to make clear that all his life Mr. Tarkington has been a "great hand" at the singing. Just the other day, in an Indianapolis paper it was reported that, under an indoor bower of greenery and in company with a number of others in fancy dress, he sang at an entertainment given for the "benefit" of something or other. It is not improbable that he is singing somewhere to-night.

A most conspicuous effect of the atmosphere of his college life which Mr. Tarkington, with amusing unconsciousness of it, has carried over into his work is the spirit of the Glee Club, an ever recurrent echo of the sound of singing. With amusing unconsciousness of it, as, when it was mentioned to him that he had an extraordinary amount of singing in his books, he first looked startled, and then collapsed as though in relish of a joke on himself.

A gentleman of the name of Lord Gomme one-time wrote a learned paper on the subject of the songs men have been wont to sing at their labors. And Mr. Belloc, in a characteristic and charming essay, has lamented the fact that Englishmen no longer sing at their rows. It would be hard indeed, I think, to find a novelist in whose works there is so much singing as in the stories of Mr. Tarkington; and a study of the songs of Mr. Tarkington ought to make a pleasant paper to be read at a literary club.

Mr. Tarkington's lovers sing; and, of all lovers, all the world must love most a singing lover. Throughout his pages "serenaders nightly seek the garden with instrumental plunkings." Or, there is wafted to the ear of the rapt one without the music of a clear, soft voice within welling the "Angels' Serenade." His drunken men sing,—and that is about the most winning thing a drunken man can do. His Sunday-school classes sing; sometimes, as in *The Flirt*, the little voices raised in:

> Prashus joowuls, sweet joowuls, *thee* jams of iz crowowun,

sing with rousing effect on the neighbors. Those of his characters who would mock sing, as Cora Madison sang of Lolita's kiss, to the horror of Hedrick. His mobs march singing "*John Brown's Body.*" Even his dead men awake and sing,—did not Tom Meredith bending over the mangled body of the supposed Teller hear, "like the sound of some far, halting minstrelsy":

> Wave willows—murmur waters—golden sunbeams smile,
> Earthly music — cannot waken — lovely — Annie Lisle?

His small boys sing and whistle with equal eloquence. And, best of all, his colored people everywhere sing as only colored people can. "When the daylight was all gone, and the stars had crept out" (in *The Gentleman from Indiana*), "strolling negroes patrolled the sidewalks, thrumming mandolins and guitars, and others came and went, singing, making the night Venetian."

The effect of this atmosphere of singing in Mr. Tarkington's books is several fold. It has a part in the success with which the author carries across the pages of his romances the glamorous spirit of chivalry. It aids greatly in giving to many of his books the infectious air which they have of youth and the "good old summer time"; people do not perhaps sing so much in winter—though it was a cold night (without) when Mr. O'Donnell at the King George Inn (in *Cherry*) led the chorus to his favorite song of the road, "The Old Bold Boy." Mr. Tarkington's portraits of humorous natures—darkies and boys—are rendered much more rounded and complete, than they would otherwise be, by his presentation of their frequent vocal flights. And, too, in his realistic pictures, the happiness, which he interprets, dwelling in small places—places of shaded streets and quiet evenings—is in no inconsiderable degree conveyed by the sounds of music flung to the air. People probably are not so much inclined to sing in great, crushing cities: it will be noted with interest that there is little or no singing in *The Turmoil;* only by the "great Thane," who, in his baronial glory, insists on roaring half-remembered fragments of "Nancy Lee" and bellowing the tune of "Larboard Watch." No, Bibbs sings his Wild Mustang song.

Sometimes, too, in his romantic moments, it will be noticed that Mr. Tarkington's musical offerings tend to produce a somewhat theatrical effect; there is something stagey about their presentation; and the lifted voices or the distant violins appear to be in the wings, before the characters come "on." Though where the whole piece has an artificial atmosphere, as in the case of *The Two Vanrevels,* this effect is of course not inconsistent, is, indeed, a skillful touch. Music fairly saturates the romantic air of *The Two Vanrevels.* Young gentlemen of the "Engine Company" put out warehouse fires singing the while, "Oh the noble Duke of York." The adorable giddiness of the adorable Mrs. Tanberry is greatly enhanced by her trilling, "Methought I Met a Damsel Fair." And Corporal Crailey Gray dies joyfully to the sound of the band's playing his favorite air of "Rosin the Bow." You observe, too, that when you dance in Mr. Tarkington's pages (and you dance there a good deal), you frequently dance to music the words of which are fully printed out for you.

The snatches of song which his characters sing, however, are not merely printed out on the story's page. These people really do *sing!* You can hear them as plain as anything. You remember that invalids murmured pitifully, and people trying to think cursed the day that they were born, when Penrod went by shrilling:

> One evuning I was sturow-ling
>   Midst the city of the *Dead*,
> I viewed where all a-round me
>   Their *peace*-full graves was SPREAD.
> But that which touched me mostlay——

Don't you *hear* that?

The acoustic properties of the songs in Mr. Tarkington's pages apparently reside in the sureness with which he seizes upon and the relish with which he stresses idiosyncrasies of pronunciation. His songs, and his dialect, are given with the energy of a kind of impish mimicry. The business upon which we are engaged in this essay, the effort to (in Mr. James' happy phrase) "catch a talent in the fact," to follow its line, and put a finger upon its essence, requires us to, so to put it, "take the finger prints" of the actor as well as of the singer in Mr. Tarkington. The mimic, the actor, is everywhere apparent in his work. He has had, from the first (as we've seen), considerable experience of the stage; he has chosen many of his closest friends from among actors; and references by the way throughout his books to the psychology and the point of view of the actor are frequent: Senator Rawson, in the story "Mrs. Protheroe," offered, on the evening of the Governor's Reception, an impression so haggard and worn that "an actor might have studied him for a make-up as a young statesman going into a decline." And Mr. Tarkington has a book to come (I've heard) which is largely a frolicking study of the actor's temperament. Also, in his personal appearance at about the time of the publication of *The Gentleman from Indiana* he was said to bear a striking resemblance to Edwin Booth's youthful pictures,—though I have seen one early photograph of about that time in which he presents (in a Noah's-ark-figure coat) decidedly the effect of a young, provincial, Methodist preacher. Perhaps it was the coat.

III

AT the end of Mr. Tarkington's junior year he was chosen as one of the editors of the *Nassau Literary Magazine*. His contributions to college periodicals may be described as in general "genteel" fragments. During his senior year he was active in forming the Coffee House Club, composed of some half-dozen members who met "to study literature." Just what was the nature of the literature studied I have not the means at hand to say; but there is internal evidence in Mr. Tarkington's literary productions now extant, of that period and the period immediately following, which strongly suggests that it was literature with a Coffee House capital C. Mr. Tarkington's pronounced early taste for a delicate flavor of the antique is fairly indicated in that one of his fledgling productions which has had the widest aftermath currency. This, a contribution in 1896 to the magazine *John-a-Dreams*, is:

A Letter of Regrets

(Left at Gilef's Coffee-Houfe; to be Given by ye Waiter to M^r. Richard Rakell, Sir Thomas Wilding, or Lord Townbrake.)

And its first stanza runs:

> Dear Rick, Sir Tom, & Will: I write
> To fay I cannot come
> To join you in ye toasts to-night;—
> I 'tend My Lady's Drum.

Rakell, Wilding, and Townbrake, one is charmed to greet as gentlemen, or at least as gentlemen having the names of gentlemen, who were cronies of his Grace of Winterset, rival of Monsieur *Beaucaire* for the heart of the *Beauty* of *Bath*, Lady Mary Carlisle. From the first, one notes, Mr. Tarkington has displayed a nice instinct for names for his people. His names never carry the slightest suggestion of the crude device of the tag: he never calls a fat man Mr. Paunch, or a miser Mr. Skinflint; yet in some subtle, happy way his names invariably do "go with" the characters of the persons that bear them, just as Mr. Pickwick is a good name for Mr. Pickwick, Tom Sawyer a good name for Tom Sawyer, and Don Quixote a good name for the immortal knight. Why is Robinson Crusoe a good name for Robinson Crusoe, and Rip Van Winkle a good name for Rip Van Winkle, and Hamlet a good name for Hamlet? I don't know. (Neither do you.) But they are good names, you will admit. And good names, too, in their way, are: Mr. Sudgeberry, John Harkless, William Sylvanus Baxter, Hector J. Ransom, Alonzo Rawson, May Parcher, Joe Bullitt,

Mr. George Crooper (the "big, fat lummox"), Judge Pike, Eskew Arp, Bibbs, Bob Skillett, and so on and many more. Sometimes, too, it will be noted, Mr. Tarkington employs in his names a graceful literary suggestion, as in Joe Louden's "airy Spirit," Ariel; and the ominous connotation of the name "Claudine" startled Miss Tabor in Joe's office, and "the sense of a mysterious catastrophe oppressed her" in regard to Mrs. Fear.

One of Mr. Tarkington's admirers has observed that "A Letter of Regrets" is as sympathetic to the spirit of its inspiration as Eugene Field's appreciations of Horace; and it would be a curmudgeon disposition that would quarrel with the observation. The point which particularly solicits attention, in the light of his later development, is that Mr. Tarkington's early inspiration was almost always purely historical and distinctly "literary." A thing natural enough. Jack London, whose "campus" was the San Francisco wharves, and their low doggeries, doubtless was somewhat oblivious of the romance of the days of powder, patches and perukes. But you wouldn't expect a normal college boy to be a very stern realist. He hasn't, particularly if he's one of the gilded youth, mentally seen any realism in life. He lives in an air of glamorous sentiment; life comes to him in terms of romance; and his æsthetic appreciation, if he have any, usually is an artistic perception of swashbuckle days. Mr. Tarkington, it is further to be noted, was thoroughly "normal," in other words even ordinary, in the matter of the period whose romance and literary flavor appealed to him above all others. Y^e-Olde-Cheshire-Cheese kind of thing is, of course, the most popular "quaintness" going. Another literary youth, Anatole France, felt that the spice of all romance was in the early lives of the saints: his Monsieur Beaucaire was Simeon Stylites.

Though the extraordinary dual nature in Mr. Tarkington, which we have here to trace, was even then operative. He has been, apparently from the first, now out-and-out romanticist, now flatly the realist,—and at times has attempted to make oil and water mix. One of the most directly observed of the realistic chapters of *The Gentleman from Indiana*, the circus scene, appeared in an early version in one of the college publications when the author was still an undergraduate at Princeton. And this incident, I should say, early proved the naturally masculine quality of his mind.

He was a consistent contributor, however, to the magazine *John-a-Dreams* during the years 1896 and 1897. This was a pleasant magazine for the sophisticated—one might say, the decadent—taste; and was exactly the type of magazine which is the last thing in the world with which we associate Mr.

Tarkington to-day. It had about it just about everything that the general public would not care for. *John-a-Dreams* announced itself on the cover as "a magazine for the conservative iconoclast and the practical dreamer." And it was, so its cover said, "devoted to mere literature and to classical typography." It was issued "about" the fifteenth of each month. "Mr. Dreams" (the magazine professed to "have no editor") declared, in "John-a-Dreams, His Ad," that he never expected "to have 'a phenominal circulation' for his magazine." As "in printing it, he does not take Barbarians, Philistines, or Populace into account." Contributions and "suggestive correspondence" were solicited from "all true lovers of literature." *John-a-Dreams* had a very polished way of saying that it did not pay for "contributions." Accepted articles, "though protected during issue by copyright," were to be "strictly regarded as the property of the author and as merely loaned to the magazine for one appearance." It was the wish of the persons in charge of the venture (whatever title they may have given themselves) that articles were to be anonymous or pseudonymous.

Articles and pieces for *John-a-Dreams* were accepted "in accordance with no canons save those of purest literary art"; "without reference to the name or fame of the author; without any pandering to the 'popular' taste; and without any consideration of commercial value." The aim was "to do something for literature rather than with it." The magazine announced that it "must depend for its existence upon the interest and aid of a small class friendly to its ideals who may make it their own medium, a sort of literary masquerade that shall completely hoodwink the critics." It trusted that it would be able to "defray its own expenses." It insisted on itself writing the "copy" of all its advertisers, among whom were numbered such of its (likewise vanished) contemporaries as *Chapters, A Monthly Magazine Devoted to Phases of Education and the By-ways of Literature*, and *The Month, In Literature, Art and Life: A Journal of Cultivation*. Privately printed poetry, of "a vagrant and impulsive muse," intended for "the lover of *belles-lettres* and the collector of limited *editions de luxe*" were chief among the merchandise advertised. This, "one of the intimately personal magazines of the day," as the Brooklyn *Eagle* called it, was, of course, "printed at ye sign" of such-and-such a "prefs" for "ye publishers." It was æsthetically bound in paper varying with each issue, sometimes the kind of paper in which meat is wrapped, sometimes in the kind which used to be "laid" under carpets. A prototype, in may respects, of this magazine which whimsically took as its name the term of "a dull and muddy-mettled rascal" in *Hamlet*.

Like John-a-Dreams, unpregnant of my cause,
And can say nothing——,

was, of course, the periodical issued by Washington Irving and his brother-in-law, "youths to fortune and to fame unknown," and called *Salmagundi*. It was a magazine of the kind which in their individual lives are as perishable as the daffodils, but of which the type apparently is immortal.

John-a-Dreams opened with *The Stirrup Cup:* "a dramatic vignette"; the scene:—tavern yard, France, sixteenth century. This was shortly followed by "A Pagan Love Song"; and a bit later by another "dramatic vignette," *The Dark Way.* Mr. Tarkington's contributions consisted both of illustrations and of some of the "pure literature." He held the purely honorary position of staff artist, and, because he disclaimed all ability to draw, he was permitted to sign his sketches with his real name. But as he made some pretensions to an ability to write, he was compelled to sign all his literary contributions with the *nom de plume* "Cecil Woodford." The author, sometime later, of *Penrod* is found writing a poem, from the French of Baudelaire, "Love on the Skull." The most ambitious of Mr. Tarkington's *John-a-Dreams* pieces, and the most Tarkingtonian was his little one-act comedy called *The Kisses of Marjorie*, later pirated by a Western newspaper. The scene is laid in "Mrs. Mellowe's rose garden," Philadelphia, 1778. And the slender action of the piece is concerned with the coming, disguised, of Captain William Lawrence, aide-de-camp to Light Horse Lee, to a dance in order to see his sweetheart, Miss Marjorie Mellowes.

As he is taking a tender farewell in the garden, he is discovered by Major McCurdy of His British Majesty's Foot, who is himself languishing for the fair Marjorie. At the critical moment Miss Marjorie "throws her arms about the Major's neck and kisses him twice, full upon the mouth." She then flies from him, and he, "breaking much crockery," pursues her around the garden for a time sufficient for Lawrence to make his escape. Then she rushes into the house and slams the door in his face. This brings the Major to himself, and, too late, he gives the alarm. The company dash from the house:

All (*shouting*): What is it? What is the matter? What has happened? Where is he? Who was it? What does it mean? What is the matter?

Maj. (*in a voice falsetto with its strain of agony*): Matter! Means! It means that an officer of Washington's dragoons—a damned rebel spy!—has been spending the evening here—

All: What!

Maj. (*gasping with rage*): Ay, under our very noses! Dancing, making love—a damned botanical villain!—and escaped—gone—flown—fled—that infernal Faversham—Haversham—Henderson.

Mrs. Mellowes: He! Can it be possible! No one could have dreamed it! How I have been deceived in the wretch!

Maj. (*with a burst of awful laughter*): Ha, ha, ha! So was I, madam—so was I! Ha, ha!

(Dorothy *comes running from the house, white-faced, calling to* Mrs. Mellowes.)

Dorothy: Mother, mother, mother! Cousin Marjorie hath gone mad! She hath gone mad! She came leaping up stairs, weeping and screaming and laughing dementedly, and calling for a bucket of water, she plunged her whole head in it a dozen times, madly, oh, so madly—her hair pasted and powdered and done as it was—until she is dreadful to see; and now she lies upon the bed and rubs her face with a great, rough towel, crying out: "The wine-bibber, oh, oh, the wine-bibber!" Haste to her before she dies.

(*The Major opens his mouth to speak, but no sound comes from it. He leans against the garden wall. Ensign Gay's eyes rest on him strangely. The Major's eyes refuse to meet the eyes of Ensign Gay.*)

Curtain.

The Kisses of Marjorie, it will be seen, has a measure of the Tarkington bouquet. At the time the little play was written Mr. Tarkington had a "hunch" that he could write a play for Richard Mansfield, and was having one effort after another "turned down" by that ornament of our stage. The main point, however, of *The Kisses of Marjorie* is the lucky part it played in the inscrutable workings of a young man's destiny. Mr. Tarkington made a number of drawings to accompany the play as illustrations in the magazine. And, as has often been told, from one of these—that one of which the caption runs, "The Major's eyes refuse to meet the eyes of Ensign Gay"—as the original lay on his desk and his fancy kept playing about it, he spun a romance into which the character with which he had endowed the little figures of the drawing would fit. Then (those were indeed the days of an amateur of the arts) this romance, *Monsieur Beaucaire* (it is said), lay in his desk two years before being sent to a publisher.

Mr. Tarkington's early drawings, of which numerous specimens have been fondly exhibited in divers magazine sketches of the author, pique a more critical attention than has before been given them. They show, very nearly, as small an ability as Thackcray's. Certain it is that a stern instructor at, say, the Art Students' League of New York, would not see in them the stroke of a student of any rare promise. It is amusing, if no more, to observe that Mr. Tarkington's drawings, like his writings, are in two distinctly different veins: some are conceived in the spirit of historical romanticism, and others in the spirit of realistic satire. His little set pieces, in the romantic vein, in which he really tried, and which combine a sort of Edwin Abbey sentiment with, very faintly, a kind of Du Maurier quality, are curiously feeble. The *flair* for human characterization by a pencil displayed by Mr. Chesterton fairly nonpluses the beholder instructed in the perception of such talent. And it seems a bit strange that an eye which will give you such a glimpse in prose as this from *The Flirt:*

He was a slender young man in hot black clothes; he wore the unfaçaded collar fatally and unanimously adopted by all adam's-apple men of morals; he was washed, fair, flat-skulled, clean-minded, and industrious; and the only noise of any kind he ever made in the world was on Sunday—in Sunday-school,

should be so futile in grasp of character as Mr. Tarkington appears in his little "illustrations." While some of the drawings which he used to make —there pops into one's head one in particular, called "By-gone cheer"—had a bright effect of animation, they were in general (one must confess) stiff in drawing, "tight," timid, effeminate. That is, his rather ambitious little designs in romantic vein. His hasty scrawls in caricature of himself, frequent marginalia to his intimate letters, have strength and considerable spiritedness, and a good deal of jovial humor. In these is about the only place in his drawing wherein is revealed any perception of character. Mr. Tarkington's physiognomy is about as inviting to caricature as that of the late Phil May's, and there is in his self-caricatures something of the Phil-Mayian relish of the artist's own humorous appearance. For what it may be worth in the way of suggestion, it should be noted that as a draughtsman Mr. Tarkington's forte was, or is, in satire. Of course, it is very "nice" that Mr. Tarkington liked to "draw," and (though it is difficult to say exactly why) everybody likes him the better for it; but, the upshot of the matter is, it is perfectly splendid that he concluded that he couldn't.

It was in 1893, before his *John-a-Dreams* pleasautries, that Mr. Tarkington took his degree of A. M. at Princeton, and went from his *alma mater* with (so-the story goes) something of a general understanding round about him that he was to devote himself to literary work. Naturally, it is reported, there were many of his own class, and some of maturer years, who looked for almost immediate achievement. And it is not unlikely that he himself may have entertained the immemorial notion of meteoric youth, that the world was already his oyster. Doubtless, as Mr. Arthur Bartlett Maurice conjectures in his article on Mr. Tarkington in *The Bookman* of a number of years ago, there was something of Mr. Tarkington's own disillusionment in his description of John Harkless, "the Great Harkless," occupied with a realization that "there had been a man in his class whose ambition needed no restraint, his promise was so complete—in the strong belief of the University, a belief that he could not help knowing—and that seven years to a day from his Commencement this man was sitting on a fence rail in Indiana." And Mr. Maurice adds, "sitting on a rail-fence in Indiana was figuratively just what Tarkington was doing from 1893 to 1899." Just so. Though, all in all, it was a decidedly figurative fence-rail.

Mr. Tarkington might have said with quite as much truth as Stevenson, "All through my boyhood and youth, I was known and pointed out for the pattern of an idler." Indeed, until in the neighborhood of his thirtieth year his career seems to have been regarded by his fellow-townsmen in the light of a rather attractive joke. He was "a big duck in the puddle" in all affairs of "society" in his home town. A young man of fashion, quite the young man about town, he served a hard schooling indeed in the life of balls and "junketings" which so frequently lights the scene in his stories. Especially did he "ride a high horse" in the goings-on of the local Dramatic Club. His principal visible business, according to old rumor, was gallant courtesy to every visiting petticoat of quality. According to an old classmate, he was (then) "a romanticist in life as in literature."

And yet, equally with R. L. S., this other "idler," too, was always busy on his own private end, which was—not an ordinary thing to-day—"to learn to write." Those roving in the nocturnal depths past the Tarkington homestead at that period of the idler's business remarked what, if they had then thought of it that way, was the mark of a late student: the lamp at midnight hour, seen in the high, lonely tower, which did oft' outwatch the well-known *Bear*, and so on. It was probably a consciousness of the foolish look which his unrewarded activities may have had outside that caused Mr. Tarkington at that time modestly to describe the serious schooling which he gave himself as "fussin' with literachoor."

Much of what he wrote at that time, one gathers from him, was for no definite ulterior use; it was written consciously for practice, or perhaps done unconscious of that aim. The symptoms are the readily recognizable ones of the birth throes of an innate vocation. It was not so much that he wished to be an author (though he wished that too) as that instinct impelled him to acquire proficiency in the art of writing, just as instinct moves a cat to look out for rats, and a horse to decline meat. Like that other "idle apprentice," he industriously "played the sedulous ape" to many and diverse masters. Whenever he read a book or a passage that particularly struck him he, too, must straightway react to it in imitation of it, or in satire upon it. He gave a story of this time to Riley, without comment, to learn "what was the matter with it." Riley went through the manuscript carefully "correcting" archaisms, until he could stand his exasperation no longer, when upon the margin he denounced the whole thing as "pure Goldsmith." And so, of course, the young student of the style of the eighteenth century (that most literary of centuries which lays its spell upon all young, ardent spirits) had designed his story to be. A dodge in impersonation, it was; a "purely ventriloquial effort," as that other "sedulous ape" said of his "monkey tricks" after the manner, in turn, of a fearful medley of masters, from Sir Thomas Browne to Swinburne.

"Writing like a streak" has never yet "come natural." Mr. Tarkington's testimony is that of all artists. "There are no teachers," he says, looking hard into his past. "We must work it out alone. We must learn by failure and by repeated efforts how the thing should be done." If for no other reason than because of the salutary effect attention to his preliminary proceedings should have upon a host of those who aspire to become authors over night, there is, it may be submitted, occasion for a handy guide (such as this) to the methods of one of the most highly rewarded, most representative, least "literary," and most "modern" of our writers. The author of the Lucius Brutus Allen stories is perceived learning his trade quite in the manner practised by the painters and craftsmen of old, patiently equipping himself in the classic way, by a painstaking interrogation of the secrets of the masters of the past. He "practised the literary scales," as the author of *Memories and Portraits* says; who adds: "That, like it or not, is the way to learn to write:"

It is only after years of such gymnastic that one can sit down at last, legions of words swarming to his call, dozens of turns of phrase simultaneously bidding for his choice, and he himself knowing what he wants to do and (within the narrow limit of a man's ability) able to do it.

Within the narrow limit of his ability, Mr. Tarkington to-day, I have heard it vowed, can on occasion write 10,000 words in a day.

Anyone whose business it has been (for his sins) to review the muck of books from morning till night, or any whose travail it is to be a publisher's reader, will tell you that it is easy writing that makes his life one of hard reading, that the absence among American authors of the result of the "gymnastic" which gives facility of expression is lamentable and extraordinary. Everyone does not consciously feel the charm of a thing by which Mr. Tarkington sets much store, the *way in which a book is written.* But everyone does like his reading to be clear, easy to understand. Mr. Tarkington's style is a curiously fluid one, which changes its color with every turn; but in this, in clarity, conspicuous among our authors, popular and unpopular, he has seldom failed to bless his reader.

It is the creed of a celebrated French master that it is the author's business to make truth beautiful, and nothing is beautiful but what is easy in its effect; that an artist who knows his trade will "not so much exact attention as surprise it"; and that obscurity, difficulty, is but a kind of bad manners. "Elegant, facile, rapid," he says, "there you have the perfect politeness of a writer." In sum, Mr. Tarkington's style, with all its complete modernity to-day, is such a style as comes of good breeding, of having early assimilated the atmosphere of the best literary society, that is of first-rate writers. Neatness, precision, ease, moderation, lightness of touch, lucidity, these, in general, are its qualities. He is clever without being smart, and pointed without emphasis. As for that dreadful something which goes by the name of rhetoric, you may search his volumes through without finding a trace of it.

Brilliancy, surprise, felicities, originalities,—all these he "wears like a flower." The qualities which, in general, form the basis of his changing style, the way in which his various books are written, occur to one as the classical French qualities. And so, it is interesting to note that of thirteen "favorite authors" which he has named, no less than four are Frenchmen: Cherbuliez, Daudet, Balzac, and Dumas. He has said that he reads more autobiography, preferably French, than anything else.

As an apprentice, of course, Mr. Tarkington "had the drop on" a good many; he had plenty of time; there was no hurry. Among other things, he learned pretty well, from his seat on the fence rail, that, unlike *John-a-Dreams*, which depended for its existence "upon a small class friendly to its ideals," magazines which make a business of being magazines do consider the "popular" taste and take thought of the "commercial value" of work purchased. In the course of time, his grasp on this idea surpassed in an astonishing way that of most young men who make a *John-a-Dreams*, or London-Poetry-Shop, or Greenwich-Village-Garret kind of a beginning. Though the character of the *littérateur*, which becomes an abiding shell for some who enter it, was with Mr. Tarkington but a sort of "chambered nautilus." He wrote and re-wrote his experiments, which were "rejected every time"; and he has confessed that the gross return from his first five years of effort was exactly $22.50.

Monsieur Beaucaire—in preparation for writing which, its publishers used to announce (before Mr. Tarkington stopped it), the author read forty books—for long failed to "get across." And a diary which Mr. Tarkington's father used to keep contains repeated entries stating the return of *The Gentleman from Indiana* from such or such a publishing house. At length, Mr. McClure was prevailed upon to "see" it. For eight years Mr. Tarkington had, so to put it, served for Rachel.

IV

WITH what is termed the New School of "young English realists" in our eye, it is an interesting thing to do to turn back for a glance at a type of native novel which was all the go with us at about the time when the nineteenth century was going out and the present century coming in. Among these early imitations (paradoxically speaking) of the latest thing in fiction one finds such one-time "best-sellers" as Brand Whitlock's *Thirteenth District*, Mr. Tarkington's *Gentleman from Indiana*, *The Virginians* of Owen Wister, and, coming after these, *The Pit* and *The Octopus* of Frank Norris. Devotees of the importations of the "new crowd," Walpole, Onions, Gilbert Cannan, Beresford, and the rest, should find something fascinatingly fresh about the manner of much of one, in particular, of these now more or less retired American novels, one published in 1899, *The Gentleman from Indiana*.

If Plattville, Carlow County, were situated off the Tottenham Court Road, or if it were somewhere in, say, Cornwall; if the Palace Hotel bore the aromatic name of The Bending Mule, or some such thing; then in many respects Plattville's chronicle would be decidedly in the literary fashion of the last several years. Though, indeed, to complete this effect the very open and elementary character of the amateur country editor of the *Carlow County Herald* ought to be that of an author of introspective tendencies and psychological temper whose work can command the attention only of the "thoughtful." At any rate, the young Indiana author began his book in the most approved method of recent realism: that of simply opening his eyes and setting down what he saw, and what he thought about the things that he saw, together with an infusion of autobiographic imagination. Mr. Tarkington had the recipe all right, but he was unable to sustain the pedestrian mood.

Perhaps he feared he would be dull. One English reviewer, writing in the *Saturday Review*, remarked that Mr. Tarkington had set himself to depict "the irredeemable dulness of provincial life in the United States," and that his "success was phenomenal." While it should be added that another, and more critical writer, laid stress, in the *Academy*, on the "continual surprising wittiness" of the book. "Wittiness" is the word, if but one word could be used, to ticket the outstanding attraction of *The Gentleman from Indiana*. Not only does the narrative crackle with wit, but the village worthies themselves (the "human society" which gave the *Saturday*

Review-er such an "ineffaceable impression of dreariness") frequently speak in dialogue, in their own peculiar idiom, with something of the high sparkle of the characters in *The Importance of Being Ernest*. With the passing of the years the *character* of Mr. Tarkington's wit has greatly changed. The searing flashes of *The Turmoil* are far from the playful twinkle of *The Gentleman from Indiana*. But, throughout his work, if he had no other distinction, he should, I think it is safe to say, bear that of the wittiest of our novelists.

The author of *The Gentleman from Indiana* had several things on his chest to speak. The soundest of his inspirations was the impulse to paint a sympathetic picture of contemporary life in the Ohio valley. He presented the semi-urban type celebrated in Riley verse. And he stood with the Hoosier poet as the exponent of a Hoosier, kindly, generous, humorous, as idiosyncratic of the soil as the Wessex peasants of Hardy, and essentially domestic. As a realist the future iconoclastic author of *The Turmoil* began as a thoroughly sympathetic fictional historian. His mood was that which was the mode among Hoosier writers, one of enthusiastic appreciation. The author of *The Gentleman from Indiana* entered the procession of authors of a local literature that has followed the progressive years of the life of the Hoosier community; a story begun by

Dr. Edward Eggleston, and which has been continued by Miss Anna Nicholas, author of *An Idyl of the Wabash*, by Riley, Mr. Meredith Nicholson, and again Mr. Tarkington, each adding valuable and instructive chapters.

The distinctive character of Plattville as a "county seat" of the central West at the time of the story is well established; and its provincial indolence, rustic amiability, and mammoth "civic" pride are reflected with a sentimental fidelity. Mr. Tarkington presented a perfect appreciation of the strength of local affection in the simon-pure Hoosier, who goes away mainly for the joy of getting back home again; and of the thoroughly American absorption in politics which seems to be more marked in county seats of a few thousand inhabitants than in large cities, and more marked in the Hoosier than in any other "critter" under the sun, as "a Hoosier will talk politics after he is dead." The author was well with the statisticians in emphasizing the homogeneity of the Middle Western folk of the period. The people of Plattville live together like a great, kind family, who are sufficient unto themselves, and content with their own:

It would have moved their surprise as much as their indignation to hear themselves spoken of as a "secluded community"; for they sat up all night to hear the vote of New York, every campaign.

Once when the President visited Rouen, seventy miles away, there were only a few bankrupts (and not a baby amongst them) left in the deserted homes of Carlow County.

All this "happy, happy time," too, was before the day of the great "smoke," which since has steadily been darkening the Indiana sky in (and out of) Mr. Tarkington's stories, until in towns that sky has become "so despised, and maltreated there, that from early October to mid-May it is impossible for men to remember that blue is the rightful color overhead." In Plattville, remember, in the days when John Harkless was editor of the *Carlow County Herald*, there were no skies half so beautiful, nor any so "sociable," as Indiana skies:

——— Skies as blue
As the eyes of children when they smile at you.

One of the peculiarities of Indiana literature is that to the stranger, particularly to the "unagrarian Eastern traveller," the effect of the Indiana landscape is one of dreary monotony, of depressing dullness; and yet practically every Hoosier writer of any note at all, from Dr. Eggleston on, has been to a marked degree sensitive to the loveliness of his landscape, and has had an artistic feeling for weather. Except in a very few places, the Indiana landscape certainly is totally without "scenery." As it is without grandeur, so it is without intriguing charms. But, it is clear, to those that love it, its face is that of a plain, kind, old friend. And a relationship may be fancied between it and the homely rural Hoosier dialect, and so, too, between it and the simple virtues of the pioneers, and the instinct universal among the people for a plain, level-headed "philosophy." At any rate, it does seem to have had a kind of moral influence on the native literature.

The whole Indiana school of writers might fancifully be distinguished by the sobriquet of the American "landscape school," amusingly suggestive of the "little masters" of flat Holland. No Indiana writer, perhaps, has had more of a painter's eye for landscape or a poet's heart for weather than the author of *The Gentleman from Indiana*. In this book the homely beauty of pastures, level fields, quiet meadows and woodlands, and the broad flat lands which stretch out "as though the whole earth were before one," is everywhere felt, and with a touch of nobility which is one of the distinctions of the book. This is quite like a canvas that might be seen in the studio of one of the Hoosier group of painters, Mr. T. C. Steele, or Mr. Otto Stark:

He felt the light and life about him; heard the clatter of the blackbirds above him; heard the homing bees hum by, and saw the vista of white road and level landscape, framed on two sides by the branches of the grove, a vista of infinitely stretching fields of green, lined here and there with woodlands and flat to the horizon line, the village lying in their lap. No roll of meadow, no rise of pasture land, relieved their serenity nor shouldered up from them to be called a hill. A second great flock of blackbirds was settling down over the Plattville maples. As they hung in the fair dome of the sky below the few white clouds, it occurred to Harkless that some supping god had inadvertently peppered his custard, and now inverted and emptied his gigantic blue dish upon the earth, the innumerable little black dots seeming to poise for a moment, then floating slowly down from the heights.

Mr. Tarkington was not so fortunate as Conrad in *Victory* in having handy a volcano to smoulder in the background of the scene of his wild tragedy, but he too set the stage of his night drama, the attack of the White Caps on John Harkless, with a first-rate bit of dramatic weather.

Another characteristic trait of the Indiana author is his gladness in the earth's bountiful yield for the sustenance of man, and particularly his emotional relish for the home products of the soil.

> The frost is on the punkin,
> And the fodder's in the shock.

An Indiana novel usually "sets a good table"; and pumpkins, pawpaws, fried chicken, young "roas'n-ears," "home-grown" watermelon, hot rolls "as light as the fluff of a summer cloudlet," milk and honey, apple-butter flavored like the spices of Arabia, fragrant, flaky cherry-pie, and cool, rich, yellow cream: these are among the staples with which the reader is regaled. Despite the fare at the Palace Hotel, there are in *The Gentleman from Indiana,* one will venture to say, as "good eats" as in any novel readily at hand. There is plenty and to spare for every reader out at Judge *Briscoe's.* "Lige Willetts was a lover, yet he said he asked no better than to just go on eating that cherry pie till a sweet death overtook him."

An artistic incongruity inherent in a number of Mr. Tarkington's longer stories is, early and throughout, pronounced in his first novel: that is, characters least essential, or quite unessential to the story, are among the truest in drawing. Sometimes, as in *The Two Vanrevels,* the servant is greater (as art) than the master. One of the most memorable characters, to my mind, in *The Gentleman from Indiana,* is the most insignificant of all: red-haired Cynthy in a blue cotton gown, who at the "Palace" languidly waved over the dining table a long instrument made of clustered strips of green and yellow tissue paper fastened to a wooden wand. "With this she amiably amused the flies except at such times as the conversation proved too interesting, when she was apt to rest it on the shoulder of one of the guests." Cynthy's very natural romantic attraction to Mr. Harkless, reaching its climax in her clumsy inability to pin a flower on the lapel of his coat, is in itself material for a little play. Come to think of it, did not Mr. Israel Zangwill employ an almost identical *motif* in his *Merely Mary Ann?* Cynthy (by Harkless always called Charmion; no one knew why) is not a part of the plot, but she *is* a part of the history.

As a historian Mr. Tarkington is sound enough, too, in his lurid Cross-Roaders; who, of course, are not authentic White Caps at all, but merely a settlement of rowdies, analogous to the denizens of the tough neighborhood found in cities, and who masquerade as a vigilance committee merely for purposes of private mischief and revenge. As pointed out by Mr. Nicholson in his little study of the Hoosier commonwealth, the author follows accurately the social history of the good stock and the bad of Carlow County, illustrating the antipathy existing between the prosperous and intelligent and the idle and ignorant. The hostility between the people of Plattville and the Cross Roads element dates back to the first movement of population on the long trail from North Carolina into the Ohio valley. The Cross Roads folk had been evil and worthless in their early homes, and they carried their worst traits with them into Indiana.

Though his methods were different, the author of *The Gentleman from Indiana*, like the author of *The Turmoil* (and like the father of the English novel, Fielding), was a moralist. What, apparently, he undertook to say about a young man from the East who found himself in a somnolent Western town, where by driving himself day and night he had succeeded in instilling some sort of life into the place and at the same time had made himself the most important and respected of its citizens, and who yet was discouraged because he believed that he had the ability to succeed, but felt that he lacked the opportunity—was this little homily: that the best way to play a big part before a large audience to-morrow, is to play, with all your heart and all your soul and all your mind, your little part before your small audience to-day. The trouble was that, before he got through, the author of his first Morality Play was saying this at the top of his voice, in a regular din.

As a historian of Hoosier manners Mr. Tarkington has from the first brought to bear on his picture an element elsewhere lacking. The editor of the *Carlow County Herald* was a type of Hoosier new at that time and place; one who has little kinship with the earlier people of Eggleston, or with the Hoosier as Riley reports him. Though a native, he had experienced at an Eastern college an intellectual change "into something rich and strange," and after long absence became a pilgrim of light among his own people. Mr. Tarkington is very fond of the wanderer returned, hero or villain,—Harkless, Joe Louden, Valentine Corliss, Bibbs. And by this device he continually achieves a critical perspective for his Hoosier scene.

The historian and moralist who created John Harkless was also considerable of a sentimentalist. Mr. Harkless in his bucolic environment does a lot of young-man mooning, very sympathetically reported by the author. "This romancer of petticoats" "knew himself for a born lover; he had always been in love with someone."—"Though for five years the lover in him that had loved so often had been starved of all but dreams."—"Somewhere there was a girl whom he had never seen, who waited till he should come. She was Everything." —"The Undine danced before him through the lonely years." And so on and so on. Mr. Harkless moons, too, much pleasant, youthful dear old *alma mater* sentiment.

Mr. Harkless may not be quite so much *The Man of Feeling* as Henry Mackenzie's celebrated hero who, it will be remembered, dies from the shock he receives when a Scotch maiden of pensive face and mild hazel eyes acknowledges that she can return his love for her; but he is, of course, a thoroughly sentimental conception. A crowning touch of this is the Marcus-Aurelius-like nobility of his soul. As the "great Harkless" comes home on the "accommodation train" from his convalescence at Rouen he forgives his enemies, the Cross-Roaders, quite out of one of the "meditations" of the sublime Emperor: "There was ignorance in man, but no unkindness; were man utterly wise he were utterly kind." Mr. Tarkington's conception of fiction has ever been fundamentally the simple one of the early minstrels and troubadours, the ancient fabulists, and the forgotten spinners of the world's first nursery tales. He must have his Odysseus. He has never taken up with the Thackerayan humor, much the fashion since Meredith, of "a novel without a hero."

The "awkwardness" and "clumsy heaviness" of the style of *The Gentleman from Indiana* has been repeatedly spoken of. From the somewhat lumbering manner of *The Gentleman from Indiana* to the debonair spirit and cameo-cut sentences of *Monsieur Beaucaire* is indeed a far cry. But the garments worn by His Highness, Prince Louis-Philippe de Valois, duke of this and duke of that, and all the rest of it, and the circle in which he moved at Bath, would have ill-become John Harkless and the Plattville folk among whom he dwelt. The style of *The Gentleman from Indiana* is not artistically infelicitous; it is only fair to fancy it as very much the style of a young country editor, and so not without a certain harmony with the theme. The sentences, certainly, are frequently over-long for complete comfort to the reader, and there may be something a bit amateurish, the wordiness of a young writer, in the touch; but there is, too, an instinctive feeling for the right word, and a good deal of luck (or determination) in finding it.

Mr. Tarkington mentioned, some years ago, that of English authors he preferred Meredith, Stevenson, James, Wells, Bennett and Hardy; and Mr. Bennett, we know, is a close personal friend. In his quiet moments, in the amiable refinement of his alert observation of prosaic things, one finds throughout Mr. Tarkington's books many touches which imply an affinity of mind with Mr. James. Flashes of the Mr. James mood are particularly frequent in *The Gentleman from Indiana*. Confronted with this fact, Mr. Tarkington, with at first a surprised, and then with a sheepish look, as though having been caught in something wrong, admitted that he had read a good deal of Mr. James "at about that time." Among the guests of Mr. Meredith's party at Rouen were three or four married young couples who "had the air of remembering that they had forgotten the baby." And this, certainly, would seem to come from a very apt student of the suave master:

In the hall he removed his narrow-brimmed straw hat and presented a rotund and amiable head, from the top of which his auburn hair seemed to retire with a sense of defeat; it fell back, however, not in confusion, but in perfect order, and the sparse pink mist left upon his crown gave, by a supreme effort, an effect of arrangement, so that an imaginative observer would have declared that there was a part down the middle.

The sober half of *The Gentleman from Indiana*, that of earnest inspiration, is work of striking promise, a promise which, indeed, there has been some reason to feel the author had not until fairly recently begun altogether to fulfill. Professor Phelps, in his volume on the English novel, states his passing fear of four or five years ago "that the brilliant gifts of this Hoosier were going to be degraded to the production of the girl-model of the year."

A trait which may be taken as characteristic of Mr. Tarkington, as it appears in nearly all—except the most recent—of his novels, is particularly evident in *The Gentleman from Indiana*. The hot-footed action of many of his stories has (to the sedate mind) an effect comparable to a motion picture film worked at a bit too high a speed. The rapid march toward success of the rascally schemes of Mr. Valentine Corliss in *The Flirt* comes quickly to mind as an instance of this very high gear in the machinery of a story. And Harkless accomplishes a number of rather difficult things with perhaps too much ease and promptness. He rescues his paper from a moribund condition and makes it an institution of local pride and fame; in the twinkling of an eye he drives an unscrupulous political boss from power, and ushers in a new era of honest government; he declares war against the bad 'uns of the squalid Cross Roads, who for years have terrorized the neighborhood; and his crusade results in sending a considerable number of them "over the road." All this, of course, is not outside the range of probability; and the author fills in his body of detail with an intellectual honesty ardent,—but not incorruptible.

The spectator of Mr. Tarkington throughout his career is reminded of George Gray Barnard's sculpture, "Two natures contending within man." First one prevails, then the other. The two spirits that have made Mr. Tarkington a theatre of combat are realism and romanticism, and romanticism confused with a realistic setting is, of course, melodrama. *The Gentleman from Indiana* began, and maintained itself fairly well half way through, as a serious and valuable transcript of manners; and then it became a burst of purple glamour not of this world. Its author was like Mr. Dobson in his triolet:

Urceus Exit

I intended an Ode,
   And it turn'd to a Sonnet.
It began *à la mode*,
I intended an Ode;
But Rose cross'd the road
   In her latest new bonnet;
I intended an Ode;
   And it turn'd to a Sonnet.

As late even as *The Flirt* Mr. Tarkington has at times manifested a curious inability to, so to say, keep his eye on the ball.

In *The Gentleman from Indiana*, long before the lurid big business the tempter is felt. Harkless's picturesque bravado before Miss Sherwood, his nonchalant attitude toward the White Caps who are after him, is a bit in the taste of the top gallery. It is tall talk to stir the naïve. Though mention should be made here of one of Mr. Tarkington's very beguiling traits, a trick slyly disarming to the critic. His own intelligence has always apparently been quite awake to what he was doing; the delinquencies in art have seemed to be a matter of the will. In practically every instance throughout his stories, as he commits one of his foibles, melodramatic or sentimental, he implies a complete consciousness of the temper of what he has on foot.—"It was melodrama, wasn't it?" asked Helen Sherwood of John Harkless, of the scene of the attempted shooting of Harkless through which they had just passed.

"You may come in now. This isn't my court-house:" this, Harkless's remark to the mob in pursuit of the shell-game men, is, of course, a "gesture" spang at the gallery-god; and the reader hears the shrill emotional whistles from above. But there is plenty of sure-enough drama, not in the least to be sneezed at, in the climax struck by the clang in the night of the court-house bell, the bell that had tolled for the death of Morton, of Garfield, of Hendricks.... The bell clamored it far and near: the White Caps had got Mr. Harkless! Then the author begins to pile up the bad business, and his humor broadens into the "comic relief" supplied by the town sot Mr. Wilkerson, tearfully looking under barroom chairs for the lost Mr. Harkless.

The "John Brown's Body" procession which marches upon the Cross Roads to wipe out that unsavory settlement is one that ought to satisfy all the demands of a very warm imagination. When public suspicion as to who got John Harkless becomes divided between the White Caps and the pair of shell-men whom he had taken a leading hand in driving out of town, the ensuing situation is one of considerable dramatic fervor. The telegram from the neighboring city of Rouen pointing to the guilt of one of the shell-men, apparently now at the point of death, which heads off the lynching party; the delegation from Plattville arriving at the Rouen hospital to take the shell-man's dying confession; the mangled object's opening its eyes and speaking with the voice of Harkless:—fairly skillful craftsmanship, all this (if a bit on the mystery story order); the surprise, when it comes, is surprising; and the whole story has been worked up with a painstaking diligence of details, an ingenious effect of plausibility that (if you are not too exacting) effectually veil the underlying melodrama.

But from this point on, our fairly solid, historical old friend, *The Gentleman from Indiana*, is, as Kipling used to say, "another story." It is good fun enough, but, quite as rigorous critics of the story have already pointed out, it is sheer romanticism. The miracles which Helen Sherwood performs with Mr. Harkless's paper in his absence are—miracles indeed. "Her educational equipment for the work was far less than his; her experience, nothing." Her imposing on Harkless an idea of herself as a six footer, and a journalist with an amazingly conglomerate knowledge of drilling for oil, politics, ladies' work-baskets and currant jelly, may only be accepted as of the quality of a joke. The pranks of the office force of the *Herald*, and the jests of the very likable Schofield's Henry, though undeniably funny, are the kind of humor termed "cutting up."

And the burst of purple glory at the end, when the "Great Harkless" comes home to bands and streamers, and cheers enough to make the sensitive reader hold his ears, is a dream of a conquering hero's return, in the youthfulness of its conception even Penrodian.

All in all, however, *The Gentleman from Indiana* was, as a first novel, a famous victory. It has, in an abundant measure, the prime quality of a work of fiction: characters that, though drawn in simple lines, seem thoroughly alive; characters, by the score, in whom one cannot help feeling a warm, lovable human nature. It is a book that one is curiously bound by his own good nature to like, and to like a good deal, even with full consciousness of its violent artistic inconsistencies and abounding absurdities. It has style, even distinction, a degree of intellectual substance, and genuine, unflagging wit. Taken altogether, it remains to-day one of the most interesting and one of the most creditable novels written of bygone life in the Ohio valley. One thing was as plain as a pikestaff: this new writer had the root of the matter in him. *The Gentleman from Indiana* bespeaks attention at some considerable length for the reason that one is tempted to say that it contains in embryo the full complement of Mr. Tarkington's box of tricks. Though the truth of such a cavalier statement might be hard to prove at one or two points.

Of satire, malice, there was not a trace in the heart of the author of *The Gentleman from Indiana.*

"Look," said Helen. "Aren't they good, the dear people?"
"The beautiful people!" he answered.

On numerous pages the author almost wept with affection for the dear, good people of the broad flat lands of "home." When Mr. Tarkington wrote *The Turmoil* he felt that he was likely to be tarred and feathered and ridden on a rail by the men and women o' Marble'ead, to borrow a figure of speech. Instead, to his amazement, he was stopped on the street with words of praise. How did his early pæan strike the dwellers in his own cherished land? Sometime after the publication of *The Gentleman from Indiana*," Mr. Tarkington, in a magazine article called "Temptations of a Young Author," told patently of himself under the name of a young man called Lukens:

This young man had grown up in Colestown and he liked the people; he wrote a novel about them, bragging about them, telling all who were willing to read that the Colestown folks were the best and greatest on earth. He brought his manuscript to New York, and a publisher accepted it and printed it. Lukens was almost ashamed to go back to Colestown; he had written about it so much from his heart that he was as embarrassed as Barrie says a man is who has told another man that he likes him. When he got off the boat, the youth who drives a buckboard for the Colestown Hotel looked at him icily and said, "Well, you've got your nerve to come back here after writing that book about us!"

"What's the matter?" asked Lukens, trembling.

"You've defamed the sacred altars," said the other. "You said Colestown wasn't as big as Paris. And you never mentioned Bangor, nor Portland, nor Augusta. You said Colestown was quiet, and gave the impression that there wasn't a building in the place as big as the pyramid of Cheops."

"But there isn't!" protested the young man.

"Go on!" replied the other. "You're a traitor. *Sneak!*"

On his way through the town to his house Lukens was stoned, and the city marshal threw his baton at him. The Colestown weekly paper came out that evening (two days ahead of time) with two columns of denunciation, headed, "Treat Him With Silent Contempt or a *B*rick."

The young men of the town serenaded him all night with tin cans, dinner-bells and resined timber. Lukens was conscious of a strong temptation to remain indoors, and yielded to it.

V

IF in *The Gentleman from Indiana* Mr. Tarkington essayed a mongrel *genre*, and didn't quite "get away with" the monstrosity, in his next appearance before the world he demonstrated beyond all manner of doubt that he was born to the purple. *Monsieur Beaucaire*, first written in 1897, sent to a magazine and returned with the conventional rejection slip with which Mr. Tarkington in those days was as familiar as anybody, then rewritten, achieved book publication (after appearing in *McClure's Magazine*) in 1900. Its success was instantaneous and immense. As a contribution to the romantic school it has been described as a charming *jeu d'esprit*. And it has happily been compared with Dumas's *Three Guardsmen* as a humming-bird to an eagle; "yet" (as Professor Phelps says) "its brightness has not faded with the passing summer of romance." *Monsieur Beaucaire* was one of those very occasional bits of fiction which are absolutely *sui generis*. It was distinctive in its year in the same way *The Prisoner of Zenda* had been in its day, and the analogy has been carried further in that both in *Monsieur Beaucaire* and

Anthony Hope's prodigious success a suggestion has been found of Stevenson.

Where are the romances of yester year? In the middle '90's an extraordinary thing began to happen to English fiction. This has been variously explained. Professor Phelps, in his study of the English novel, has gathered together the facts and tells the story in very much the following words. At any rate, one man, Stevenson, appeared at just the moment when readers were either weary or disgusted with the reigning Sovereign, Realism, and who before he died had converted the English-speaking world to Romance adorned with graceful, exquisite, and shining garments. A couple of years before his ascendency, two English critics had perceived the signs of the coming high tide of romanticism. Mr. George Saintsbury and Mr. Edmund Gosse each independently predicted the coming flood. In an essay called "The Limits of Realism in Fiction" (1893), Mr. Gosse remarked: "Wherever I look I see the novel ripe for another reaction." And a bit later the reaction came into full swing. In 1894 appeared *The Ebb Tide*, *The Jungle Book*, *Perlycross*, *The Tragedy of Pudd'nhead Wilson*, *Under The Red Robe*, *My Lady Rotha*, and the story which exerted such a prodigious influence, *The Prisoner of Zenda*.

The demand for some of these books, as Professor

Phelps further traces, was so sharp and the rapidity of their circulation so remarkable, that the sales became a matter of interest to critics who were watching the public taste; and it was about this time that *The Bookman* began to publish its monthly list of best sellers. With romanticism suddenly become so fashionable naturally many young persons wrote their first attempts in fiction in this manner; and some novelists of established reputation, unwilling to be left adrift, trimmed their sails to the fresh breeze. The old masters, though their popularity decidedly waned, refused to surrender; and one, Mr. Howells, protested—in vain—against this sudden domination of romance, calling the whole thing romantic rot. The strength of the Romantic Revival drew men whose natural tastes, inclinations, and temperament were toward realism to the production of romances. Stanley Weyman suddenly shifted from an obscure Anthony-Trollope-like realism; produced in rapid succession, *The House of the Wolf*, *A Gentleman of France*, *Under the Red Robe*; and found himself one of the most famous men in the world. When the romantic wave subsided, he retired, apparently without (unlike the subject of our sketch) another shot in his locker.

Professor Phelps relates in his book his own experience on a Sunday evening in 1894 which illustrates in microcosmic manner the world's change of heart from realism to romanticism. He had just finished reading *Marcella*. Then he picked up *Under the Red Robe*. Such a glorious relief from tiresome party politics and pharisaical reformers in London, to:

MARKED CARDS!

the lie hotly given and returned, the tables and chairs overset, the rush for the dark street, the clash of swords, the parry and thrust—we're off!

Conan Doyle had already got under way in the late eighties with *Micah Clarke* and *The White Company*, and these books came fully into fashion in the nineties. Anthony Hope deserted what was probably his natural bent expressed in the *Dolly Dialogues*, and followed his romantic extravaganza, *The Prisoner of Zenda*, with *Rupert of Henzau*. The most popular productions of all this great vogue, such as *Zenda* and *Under the Red Robe*, had enormous runs on the boards as sheer melodrama.

The romantic germ crossed the ocean, and in 1902, Bliss Perry, then editor of the *Atlantic*, could write of "the present passion for historical novels." The characters of many of these costume novels talked a jargon of obsolete oaths, in a sentimental love story, with a historical royal personage as *deus ex machina*. It mattered not if their historical foundation betrayed ignorance, nor if their style was crude: scores of such books went like wildfire until the next sensation came along. As Professor Phelps (whom we are so largely quoting, or paraphrasing) points out, an especially representative example of the whole class appeared in Charles Major's *When Knighthood was in Flower*, a work distressingly lacking in distinction, which sold over five hundred thousand copies.

The author, later of books of political, religious, and social reform, novels like *The Inside of the Cup* and *A Far Country*, contributed to the romantic storm one of its most soaring rockets, *Richard Carvel*; and the author of the realistic *Honorable Peter Sterling* wrote *Janice Meredith*, which conquered the public immediately, and like so many of its kind was speedily transferred to the stage and thence to oblivion. The hue and cry was not less in the theatre than between covers; and at the height of this fashion a new version of Dumas's immortal story was put on the American stage by Mr. Sothern, and flourished mightily. Other hot favorites in fiction of the day were Mary Johnston's *To Have and To Hold*, Dr. Weir Mitchell's *Hugh Wynne*, and Maurice Thompson's *Alice of Old Vincennes*. *Monsieur Beaucaire* rode into popular favor on the crest of the romantic wave. The great Romantic Revival held out for about fifteen years, then spent itself as crazes do, and only one or two anachronisms among authors, like Jeffery Farnel, continued to wear the cape and plume.

Where are the romances of yester year? Dead as a door nail, most of them. Though indeed some of them do continue to survive, in an obscure existence like former beaux fallen upon shady days, in the cheap reprint editions of past favorites. And a very few, like *Hugh Wynne*, yet wear the dignity of enduring character. But, in general, now to run over a list of the titles of these one time pampered pets of the reading world brings such a smile as it does to recall song hits of other days: "Only a Bird in a Gilded Cage," "My Sweetheart's the Man in the Moon," and "Down Went McGinty to the Bottom of the Sea." And it is indeed interesting to remark that the briefest, lightest, and slightest in effect of all that dashing throng has been among the very, very few to retain something like its virgin flush of rose. *Monsieur Beaucaire* the world has not so willingly let die. It continues to be kept "in stock" at book stores, and sells (I am told) if not in quantities, at least right along to-day; and it is continually being "drawn" from the shelves of public libraries. There is no difficulty about the explanation: no work of perfect art is ever permitted to perish altogether. And, though perhaps a bit flamboyant in manner, I do not know that it is a particularly hazardous observation to say to *Beaucaire*:

When old age shall this generation waste,
  Thou shalt remain, in midst of other woe
Than ours, a friend to man, to whom thou say'st,
  "Beauty is truth, truth beauty,—that is all
  Ye know on earth, and all ye need to know."

At any rate, let us not be niggardly of appreciation in the presence of a tiny bit of well-nigh flawless beauty. *Monsieur Beaucaire* ought to last (let us say) as long as there is a taste for *The Master of Ballantrae.*

Monsieur Beaucaire has been compared to the art of Watteau. And this comparison, an inevitable one and a kind of inspiration, is the happiest of the many that have been made. It is a comparison which is constructive criticism. M. Camille Mauclair in his little study, both lyric and penetrating, of Watteau, speaks of those celebrated *fêtes galantes* as "tender, dazzling, and most deliciously aristocratic." Exactly so, *Beaucaire*, that vivid, pastel-like sketch of a flashing episode in the life of a "small, fair gentleman," radiant, exquisite of heart, brilliant, audacious, winningly dignified, a French duke of the royal blood at Bath in the eighteenth century; who masquerades, for his private purposes, in this resort of white-satin-sheen fashion first as a "gamblist" barber, and then as the Duc de Chateaurien, laughing in his sleeve at the dull-witted Englishman who, incited by the Duke of Winterset's personal animosity, tries to hunt him down as a *laquais;* who falls under the spell of "gold and snow and the blue sky of a lady's eye," the Beauty of Bath, —"*bellissima, divine, glorieuse!*"—and who shows by his sword that he is one "born." A tale, or something less than a tale, whose only, and complete, excuse for its being is the blitheness of its mood, the symmetry of its form, the iridescent color of its words, the swiftness of its action, and the tingling vitality of it, from start to finish; a thing of dainty wit all compact.

One of the perpetual delights of *Monsieur Beaucaire* is the crispness with which its sparkling and rapidly shifting scenes are realized. The reader actually sees as clearly as though he had before him a painting by the late Howard Pyle, or a drawing by Daniel Vierge, the picture given of the chairmen swarming in the street at Lady Malbourne's door, "where the joyous vulgar fought with muddled footmen and tipsy link-boys for places of vantage whence to catch a glimpse of quality and of raiment at its utmost. Dawn was in the east, and the guests were departing." Or, again, view that night of the "stately junket," when "all of Bath that pretended to fashion or condition was present at a *fête* at the house of a country gentleman of the neighborhood:"

There fell a clear September night, when the moon was radiant over town and country, over cobbled streets and winding roads. From the fields the mists rose slowly, and the air was mild and fragrant, while distances were white and full of mystery.

Then it was that the coach took the road with the happy Frenchman riding close to that adorable window which framed the fairest face in England, a dozen gallants riding before, when a wild halloo sounded ahead; the horn wound loudly, and, with drawn swords flashing in the moon, a party of horsemen charged down the highway, their cries blasting the night,—and the battle was joined. Or see *Beau Nash* standing "at the door of the rooms, smiling blandly upon a dainty throng in the pink of its finery and gay furbelows." Best of all, the scene in the Pump Room, where Monsieur Beaucaire's identity is disclosed by the arrival of his brother and the French Ambassador, to the consternation of his enemies and still more of the Lady Mary Carlisle, who had loved him until she was taught to scorn him as a servant,—a scene in which are mingled bright charm and subtle pathos.

He offered his hand to Lady Mary.

"Mademoiselle is fatigué. Will she honor me?"

He walked with her to the door, her hand fluttering faintly in his. From somewhere about the garments of one of them a little cloud of faded rose-leaves fell, and lay strewn on the floor behind them. He opened the door, and the lights shone on a multitude of eager faces turned toward it. There was a great hum of voices, and, over all, the fiddles wove a wandering air, a sweet French song of the *voyageur*.

He bowed very low, as, with fixed and glistening eyes, Lady Mary Carlisle, the Beauty of Bath, passed slowly by him and went out of the room.

Ye Gods! as Mr. Baxter says, *that* is the air of Romance.

* * * * *

There used to be (I have ferreted out) an elderly gentleman residing in the neighborhood of New York City whose keenest pleasure, and one which he exercised continually, was recounting the glories of existence in Terre Haute, Indiana—as it existed in the golden haze of his fond memory. Like that other being of sentiment celebrated in a Riley poem, it was his proud wont to (in retrospect):

> Boast and strut
> About the streets of Terry Hut.

And a reflection from this gentleman's rose-tinted spectacles was the inception of *The Two Vanrevels*, the story which, in order of publication, next followed *Monsieur Beaucaire*. For Mr. Tarkington's Rouen, Indiana, was Terre Haute, one of the older towns of Indiana, which, though it has not made so much noise in the world as a "literary center" as some other points in the state (Crawfordsville, for instance, the "Hoosier Athens," lovingly celebrated and oft' by Mr. Nicholson), contained in its earliest years families of marked cultivation. Lyman Abbott began his ministry in Indiana as pastor of the Congregational Church at Terre Haute. And the town has been the home of numerous distinguished politicians. Richard W. Thompson, who became Secretary of the Navy in President Hayes' cabinet, and who was also a writer of books, and Daniel W. Voorhees, the "tall sycamore of the Wabash," long a senator in Congress, and acclaimed the greatest forensic orator of his day in the Ohio valley, were both of Terre Haute. *The Two Vanrevels* is historically accurate in that among Terre Haute's most accomplished early citizens there was a distinct strain of the Southern States, and, presumably, a touch and more of the romantic flavor of Southern manners. In later days one of Terre Haute's citizens most conspicuously in the public eye has been a brewer, and in recent years the little city has come to be somewhat known as a home of political corruption.

Rouen, it will be remembered, was also only "seventy miles away" from Plattville. There it was Tom Meredith had his home, to which the convalescent John Harkless drove from the hospital in a victoria "through the pretty streets:" "a capacious house in the Western fashion of the Seventies," with, in front, on the lawn, a fountain with a leaping play of water, and maples and shrubbery everywhere. That, however, was in the Nineties.

"It was long ago in the days when men sighed when they fell in love; when people danced by candle and lamp, and did dance, too, instead of solemnly gliding about; in that mellow time so long ago, when the young were romantic and summer was roses and wine, old Carewe brought his lovely daughter home from the convent to wreck the hearts of the youth of Rouen." A reviewer in the *Athenæum* found in Mr. Tarkington's Rouen of *The Two Vanrevels*—"the leading center of elegance and culture in the Ohio valley"—"despite wide differences, something of the atmosphere of *Cranford* or of the homes of some of Jane Austen's pleasant people." The feminine society wholly in the possession of the out-of-the-way English village of Cranford before the encroachment of railways and penny postage, one fears, would have gone into hysterics had it lived through the lurid night of old Carewe's warehouse fire. And what would those widows and spinsters, who spent their time in tea-drinking and trivial gossip, and in chasing sunbeams from their carpets, who before going to bed peeped beneath the white dimity valance or rolled a ball under it, to be sure no Iachimo with "great fierce face" lay concealed there—what would they have made of that town Lothario and Light-o'-Love, romantically dissipated Crailey Gray? And Miss Austen, too, who ruffles her readers by nothing vehement, doubtless would have been thrown somewhat off her center by such a deed of blood occurring in one of her novels as the mistaken murder of the beloved vagabond gentleman in the new soldier's uniform of Tom Vanrevel.

One sees, however, what the reviewer had in mind; and it is just as well that the name of Miss Austen has been brought into the matter, as, despite the wide differences, humorously wide differences, between them, it is not difficult to fancy here and there in Mr. Tarkington's earlier work, in his vivacious transcript of manners, something amusingly Jane-Austenish about him. The provincial material with which he is so familiar and which so strongly attracts him by its flavor is very much a later-day counterpart of that of Miss Austen's. He, too, is fond of finding comedy in the amenities of youthful social life, critical amusement in the intimate contacts of the domestic circle, and the movements of fate in the play of small things. He has something of the same bubble of mind, and beneath the surface a like undercurrent of common sense and respectable thinking. And like Miss Austen's style, his is that of everyday life, to which he has added an element of charm.

Though the setting of *The Two Vanrevels* is once more Mr. Tarkington's happy hunting ground, Indiana, it is an Indiana quite unfelt by the author of *The Hoosier Schoolmaster* or the author of *The Old Swimmin'-Hole, and 'Leven-More Poems;* an Indiana, indeed, after the heart of the author of *Monsieur Beaucaire*. In this story Mr. Tarkington essayed his single historical romance of Indiana, and sought the rose-tinted mist of distance essential to a tale of this type by throwing back the time of action a couple of generations, to the days just preceding the outbreak of the Mexican war; and by peopling it with men of old-fashioned courtliness and women of gracious manners and soft-voiced charm. The author was in love with the age. It was "the age of garlands; they wreathed the Muses, the Seasons, and their speech, so women wore wreaths in their hair"; the age of brocade, ribbons and furbelows; of balls and junketings, carpet dances and masquerades; of canes, and bright buttons on men's coats, of echoes of the Beau, like Crailey Gray; when "polished manners" were the fashion, and "hospitality" meant "a house with a side-board like a widow's cruse:" "Mr. Bareaud at fifty had lived so well that he gave up walking, which did not trouble him; but at sixty he gave up dancing, which did trouble him." In this novel of high-class comedy type there is ever "a scent of flowers in the air," or "the air is heavy with roses and tremulous with June." It was a pleasant day, and, it would seem, a pleasant place to live, that Rouen, those many years ago in the Ohio valley. Mr. Tarkington, however, sought to recapture the first, fine, careless rapture of an old gentleman; and it is his own opinion that he did not succeed; his "atmosphere" being neither here nor there, but in an old gentleman's roseate memory.

The Two Vanrevels is both a better book and a poorer book than *The Gentleman from Indiana*, which in date of composition immediately preceded it. *The Two Vanrevels*, like *Monsieur Beaucaire*, is the kind of thing which depends altogether on technical excellence to be anything at all. *The Gentleman from Indiana* is the kind of book which, like that well-known recent affair, William McFee's *Casuals of the Sea*, both more of a book and more altogether formless, can stand by the substance, the stuff, that is in it. The plot structure of *The Two Vanrevels*, though slight in frame, is of artistic workmanship; the story is marked by a careful consideration of the niceties of character; and, as in *Beaucaire*, the author recognizes consistently throughout the story the key in which he is pitching his story, that of sheer romanticism, which here and there flares into mélodrama.

Fault has been found with *The Two Vanrevels* on the score of lack of plausibility. Mark Twain (wasn't it?) declared that he knew of but seven plots in the world. He was, apparently, six to the good of Mr. Tarkington's game. The basis of practically every story he has written, down to *The Turmoil*, has been a misunderstanding of one kind or another, of identity, of purpose, of character. And in repeated instances this misunderstanding has been of the most elementary sort, that of mistaken identity. This charge, however, really goes no further than to say that, like many men of the highest gift, which he has in fair measure, imagination, he is curiously feeble in the faculty of *invention*. He is no Poe. In some cases, as in *The Flirt*, ripping as a character study, his efforts at invention in the surrounding story are almost childlike. Contrary to what very likely we have been wont lightly to suppose, in the essence of his talent the play is never the thing. The people are the thing, and the freshness of the art with which the thrice-told tale is told.

It is not (as has been observed in an earlier criticism) perhaps likely that Miss Betty Carewe could have made the blunder she did in taking Tom Vanrevel and Crailey Gray each for the other in a town where everyone knew everyone else, where she was continually meeting first one of the two men and then the other, at all sorts of social functions, talking with them, dancing with them, more than liable at any moment to hear them addressed by name. In *Monsieur Beaucaire* and in *The Gentleman from Indiana*, as this former criticism noted, the same contrivance appears more natural: the identity of the Prince is an easily kept secret because it is shared by no one but his loyal servants,—and *Beaucaire* has the further advantage in this of being very brief; the identity of the substitute editor of the *Carlow County Herald* is easily concealed from the hero because Harkless is flat on his back in a hospital ward in another town seventy miles distant,— and in *The Gentleman from Indiana* there is the further advantage that the secret had to be kept throughout only a fraction of the story. The germ of *The Two Vanrevels* is said to have been a story of two thousand words written many years before; and in expanding it to serve as the excuse for a fulllength novel the author perhaps strained a device which would have served more effectively as the sub-structure of a short story. But, after all, *The Two Vanrevels* is exactly the sort of a gift-horse which it is perhaps a bit heavy in us to look in the mouth. The period of its composition was with the author, as in the atmosphere of the story, one of

June and wine and roses; and Mr. Tarkington had probably concluded at the time he wrote the book that his "job" was merely to give entertainment, and he supplied this, in *The Two Vanrevels*, with something of a *tour de force*.

In many ways the book pleasantly suggests the air of Congreve, Farquhar, Wycherley, what Elia termed the artificial comedy of last century. It invites the mood of not carrying our fireside concerns to the theatre, but of going thither, like our anecstors, to escape from the pressure of reality. Its creatures are the fictitious half-believed personages of the stage (the phantoms of old comedy); sports of a witty fancy, they seem engaged in their proper element, idle gallantry. They are not so much of Christendom, as (in Lamb's conceit) of the land of cuckoldry—the Utopia of gallantry. The curmudgeon merchant, ferocious old Carewe, the richest man and the best hater in the community, in whose opinion, loudly expressed, the law firm of Vanrevel and Gray is composed of a knave and a fool—an opinion in which he is not the slightest disturbed by the fact that the public generally has never made up its mind which of the two it loves the more: the town model of virtue, Tom Vanrevel, or lighthearted, fickle, fascinating and utterly irresponsible Crailey Gray;—gambling, murderous old Carewe is not at all convincing as a character in real life; but he does well enough as a satisfying hobgoblin. On the other hand, Mr. Tarkington's artistic failing, his great luck with minor characters, again comes to the fore in his creation of the enlivening widow, Mrs. Tanberry, "who was about sixty, looked forty, and at first you might have guessed she weighed nearly three hundred, but the lightness of her smile, and the actual buoyancy which she somehow imparted to her whole dominion lessened that by at least a hundred-weight,"—Jane Tanberry, "young Janie Tanberry," who declared to the belle of Rouen "we're the same foolish age, you know." She is indeed irresistible, and would seem to be right out of some old play like Sheridan's *Rivals*.

The town scamp and ne'er-do-well, the too, too picturesque Crailey Gray, wit, poet, and scapegrace and chief comedian of Rouen, with the "mark" upon him described by that one of his lady-loves who loved him best, Fanchon Bareaud, as a "look of fate," seems to be a sort of angelicized Sydney Carton (a character much admired by William Baxter). In his infinite capacity for flirtation he reminds one of Mr. St. Ives, who declared, "When I can't please a woman, hang me in my cravat!" If one attempts to gather from Mr. Tarkington's various heroes a sort of collective statement of the Tarkington hero, one gets—into difficulties. On one hand we have a composite portrait of, altogether, a somewhat Fieldinglike type of hero. Though they are mighty fine fellows, like Tom Jones, they are sad dogs, many of Mr. Tarkington's heroes: Crailey Gray, William Fentriss, Joe Louden, Robert Russ Mellin, Larrabee Harman, and—yes—Penrod Schofield. On the other hand, there are Saint John Harkless, Tom Vanrevel, Bibbs Sheridan, estimable gentlemen, all.

Romantically dissipated Crailey Gray (who belonged to a vanished day when John Barleycorn, now by the world degraded by the name of booze, was a gentleman of fashion, rejoicing in the society of the brightest) may seem to have little relation to Mr. Harkless; and yet there is the link of the "born lover" between them. Mr. Gray has "cared more deeply than other men for every lovely thing I ever saw," and "I'd be ashamed not to have cared for the beauty in all the women I've made love to." *The Two Vanrevels*, however, has the peculiarity of having two heroes (samples of both of Mr. Tarkington's brands), the law firm of Gray and Vanrevel; and Mr. Tarkington (scratching his head to induce clearer recollection) says he "thinks" he had in mind some such symbolic idea as that "the two Vanrevels," who complemented each other, together made one complete man.

As a swain the Tarkington hero is very—Tarkingtonian. He is bold and dashing in attack, when he thinks of the beauty to be won, and faint of heart, when he thinks of his own unworthiness. "The stupidity of these heroes," wrote Mr. Maurice in his *Bookman* article of a number of years ago, "appears the more crass in view of the simple candour that is the predominating characteristic of every one of his heroines. In fact, it is that personal directness that in almost every case is brought into play as a last resort. Helen Fisbee, Betty Carewe, and Ariel Tabor do not actually propose—in so many words. But—Ariel Tabor extends her hands to Joe Louden, bidding him take them instead of empty gloves; Betty Carewe whispers to the undiscerning Vanrevel that he is the one whom the dying Crailey Gray prophesied was to return to complete her life; Helen Fisbee, finding that conventional encouragement is of no avail, resorts to measures still more direct." And Sylvia Gray does throw herself outright into the arms of William Fentriss, crying, "Then you must just have me!" Mrs. Lindley must slyly inspire her son Richard to go to claim Laura Madison, already his for the coming. And Bibbs's father must bring his Mary Vertress to him. Yet the reader is never shocked by the suggestion of boldness in these ladies so clearly loved. What else, except shaking them, was to be done with wooers so humble minded and obtuse?

The most interesting thing about Crailey Gray,

however, to one on the trail of Mr. Tarkington, is that he was called "peculiar" by the quiet souls of Rouen. The "oddity," the "queer" one, the character of finer grain, whose actual home is not of the world about him, the social "outsider," the finely intelligent being whose higher wisdom is held by the community to indicate a lack of mental balance, the disinterested observer of the scene: this is a character dear to the heart of Mr. Tarkington. There is a long line of succession: the patriarchal Mr. Fisbee, the only inhabitant of Plattville who had an unknown past; Crailey Gray, whose poems his law partner declared were worth more than all the legal business done by the firm; the outcast Joe Louden, and the hoyden Ariel Tabor; the impoverished Italian gentleman, Ansolini; the childlike Oliver Saffren; the brilliant, tragic Ray Vilas; the sensitive invalid Bibbs Sheridan. And, though so oft repeated as to seem a part of a constructive formula, it is a device which, in union with his figure of the returned wanderer, Mr. Tarkington employs with considerable effect, most notably in the case of Bibbs, in obtaining the critical perspective, which, it is one of the points this survey of him would bring forward, his instinct has always sought.

Conrad, of course, is another who goes at his, rather more profound, statement of social values from the angle of the outsider, the outcast. But in his somber conception of life as a struggle in which man is doomed only to defeat, all of Conrad's brilliant and poignant beings are dreamers who go to smash upon the rocks of human weakness and stupidity. Most of Mr. Tarkington's earlier stories were cast in the airy optimistic traditions of the popular stage, where virtue is bound to triumph over evil, and heartily applauded courage by daring all "wins through;" but the years have very strikingly deepened his art, and into his later books has come (with little or no recognition by the reviewers) a good deal of the more pondering, Conrad note. Vilas is destroyed by the selfish heartlessness of a vain and vulgar woman, a kind of stupidity; and over *Bibbs* his enemy, the god of *Bigness*, did finally prevail.

Ancient Uncle Xenophon, rheumatic, rusty of joint, bent upon a hickory stick, who might have known the prophets, who wore that hoary look of unearthly wisdom many decades of superstitious experience sometimes give to members of his race, his face—so tortured with wrinkles that it might have been made of innumerable black threads woven together—a living mask of the mystery of his blood; —Uncle Zen, who told as one having authority where the injured John Harkless lay, was an awesome figure of a very genuine old negro of a type; but it is in *The Two Vanrevels* that Mr. Tarkington's extraordinary gift for catching the heart of the character of the Afro-American began apparently to find itself. The Carewes' old house-servant, Old Nelson, humming an old "spiritual," "Chain de Lion Down," and the cook, vain Mamie, should have honorable mention in Mr. Tarkington's extensive gallery of darkey portraits by an inspired hand.

Mr. Tarkington to-day declares, with the "look" of a man who is unpleasantly reminded of a former malady, that he "can no longer read Stevenson." In the light of the evolution of his feeling for style *The Two Vanrevels* has particular interest; nowhere else in his work is there so much a Stevensonian consciousness of the "gesture" of style, nowhere so much, as Stevenson put it, the "love of lovely words." Nothing to-day, apparently, so much gives Mr. Tarkington the horrors as the idea of the "literary." He does not want to be "caught," he declares, writing "prose." Some literary editor in New York told him that some of the passages in *The Turmoil*, in particular (I think) the cemetery scene, were noble English prose, worthy, I suppose, of the author of *Urn Burial*. "He liked them," says Mr. Tarkington, with a wry face, as though, if he knew just how, he would cut those passages out. In *The Two Vanrevels* there are even slight affectations of speech, as, once, the word "instanter," and a frequent repetition of the stylistic use of "never," as in "danced she never so hard and late," and "though never so slightly"; though of course this blend of *St. Ives* and *Godey's Magazine* kind of style is quite proper to the story. And throughout *The Two Vanrevels* there are (whether or not the author now likes them) quite charming bits of writing. It is a charming touch, Miss *Betty's* hurrying to a seat by Mrs. Tanberry, and "nestling to her like a young sapling on a hillside." The landscape painting is done with a lighter brush and a thinner pigment than in *The Gentleman from Indiana:*

Noon found Tom far out on the National Road, creaking along over the yellow dust in a light wagon, between bordering forests that smelt spicily of wet underbrush and May-apples; and, here and there, when they would emerge from the woods to cleared fields, liberally outlined by long snake-fences of black walnut, the steady, jog-trotting old horse lifted his head and looked interested in the world, but Tom never did either.

An earlier draught of *The Gentleman from Indiana*, it is told, a tale of which forty thousand words were written about a young college graduate who became a country editor in an Indiana town very much like the Plattville of the later novel, came to an abrupt end when the hero was in the middle of a walk, the author being unable to carry him a step further. A suspicion hangs in the air of *The*

Two Vanrevels that there was some fumbling in winding up that story: and the author acknowledges that there he was "stuck" again. He went away to attend to the production of a play, and upon his return it was "wonderful" that he managed to carry off the thing at all. Maybe it was the heroic effort required to end the story which led to the humorous effect of George-Cohaning at the end, where "the flag goes marching by,"—while the audience (as it is required by patriotism to do) should arise and cheer. Following *The Two Vanrevels* appeared the least understood of Mr. Tarkington's seldom esoteric stories.

* * * * ÷

It is, among other things, the business of the critic to reconcile the irreconcilable. Those numerous things in Mr. Tarkington which, seen out of their natural relation, seem inexplicable in their origin become clear enough when correlated with other things. A reader (I've heard of such) acquainted with Mr. Tarkington only through his later books who should stumble upon *Cherry* might well be flabbergasted. *Cherry*, however, is clearly the direct offspring of Mr. Tarkington's *John-a-Dreams* period.

It is a prose caricature by an exquisite in letters— and a poet. Austin Dobson might have done it in a triple roundel, or the late Andrew Lang in a ballade. It is a titbit of *belles-lettres*, a bagatelle for the epicure, a "relish" to tickle the delicate, sensitive palate; an olive for the hightly cultivated taste; to be compared to a drawing and verse by the incomparable Oliver Herford, or to be matched, say, in the "works" of the matchless Max Beerbohm. It is this for the reader—the connoisseur; for the author it was a little drill in his rigorous apprenticeship to becoming a writer that can write.

Though *Cherry* did not appear in book form until 1903, it was written before either *The Gentleman from Indiana* or *Monsieur Beaucaire;* and the amazing thing about it is—as the term "caviare to the general" certainly fits *Cherry* to a T—that it was taken, as a two part serial, by a popular magazine when its author was practically unknown. I should say that there are just about a dozen, perhaps six, people in the United States who would find their heart's delight in precisely this kind of thing. The remarkable editor who took *Cherry* on its merits as a waggish farce, a whimsical tale with a consummately polished surface like a Vermeer, later probably regarded it in the light of an unhappy selection —as an editorial *faux pas*, perhaps—until the success of the author's other books brought it quickly out of its obscurity in manuscript or galley-form, and led to swift publication with a greatly augmented value.

Cherry is extraordinary among Mr. Tarkington's

books in that the story is laid in New Jersey, in the days preceding the American Revolution. This "heroic tale of the days when Commencement came in September" is appropriately dedicated to the class of 1893 at Nassau Hall, concerning which dedication the New York *Sun* remarked doubtfully that it hoped the class would appreciate the tribute. To attempt to state the plot (as some critics have done), and thus to sever it from the envelope of atmosphere which is its life, would indeed be to break a butterfly on the wheel,—and the story would appear the extreme of mediocrity. To say, as has been said, that the story "turns on a practical joke," would be equally—Mr. Sudgeberryish. The story "turns" on its high spirits, its sportive gayety, its delicious drollery.

It may be questioned whether the "exaggerated pedantry" of Mr. Sudgeberry, who at the age of nineteen is finishing his third year of study at Nassau Hall, has not been a bit exaggerated by numerous critics of the story. Mr. Sudgeberry's pedantry of course would be quite impossible in our "red blood" day, sufficiently (in all conscience) emancipated from the fetish of "scholarship" and impatient enough of mental "improvement" as a moral virtue. But at the period when Mr. Sudgeberry flourished was not Johnsonian "learning" the fashion among callow youth? In his day, even so estimable a gentleman as John Milton was capable right along of such pomposity as this, in a letter to a friend:

> I who certainly have not merely wetted the tip of my lips in the stream of these (the classical) languages, but in proportion to my years have swallowed the most copious draughts, can yet sometimes retire with avidity and delight to feast on Dante, Petrarch, and many others; nor has Athens itself been able to confine me to the transparent waves of its Ilissus, nor ancient Rome to the banks of its Tiber, so as to prevent my visiting with delight the streams of the Arno and the hills of Faesolæ.

Mr. Sudgeberry could not go Mr. Milton much better than that. And as for the "intolerable priggishness" and the "incredible self-satisfaction," as these traits have been called, of Mr. Sudgeberry, why, the conscious righteousness of a character such as (the revered) Colonel Esmond, also a narrator in the first person, is capable of ridicule; and it may be that Mr. Tarkington had in mind the intention of writing a blithe parody, such as Fielding's *Pamela*.

At any rate, the "unbelievably" thick-headed Mr. Sudgeberry (as some readers have found him) is a prig in the Grand Manner. He tells his unfortunate love story with the unconscious satisfaction of the prig type, feeling certain of his success with the heartless Sylvia, who is laughing at him all along, and using him for the purposes of advance with her other young man. And the boisterous adventure which brings the affair to an end is an excellent bit of fun, well contrived, and told with great vivacity and a delicate art which makes the reader feel a dash of sympathy for the dupe.

The history of *Cherry* subsequent to its long withheld publication is entertaining, and is interesting, too, as a study in the psychology of the American reading public. The story, of course, is one of a kind more readily comprehended by the English taste, and, indeed, was at once much more appreciatively reviewed in the English papers than in our own. While there may be (for all I know) some so temperamentally disposed that they have placed *Cherry* on their shelves as a companion piece to *Love in Olde Cloathes* and next to *A Sentimental Journey*, the book has certainly puzzled and irritated a great many readers. The author received numerous letters from troubled souls saying they would never again read a book of his. And, apparently, Mr. Tarkington has had so "rubbed in" a notion of the incommunicability of the idea he sought to express in the little story that he now can comprehend only with difficulty that anyone "gets" it; as he solemnly explained to the present writer, and at tedious length, that the sore distressed Mr. Gray, and all the rest, were only "guying" Mr. Sudgeberry. "GUYING him!" Mr. Tarkington shouted at me, as though convinced that something like physical force was required to get the point into my head.

I recently re-read a copy of *Cherry* from a public library. A former reader of this volume had emphatically expressed himself in pencil on the title page; he gave his opinion of the book as "N. G." Still another reader of this same copy voiced his feelings at the end; under the printed word "*Finis,*" he had inscribed his hearty comment: "nuff!" The great misfortune of the author of *Cherry* was that he exercised unusual gifts as an ironist. "Thou shalt not commit irony," this, Mr. Edmund Gosse, writing somewhere on Anatole France, declares is the first commandment of the English-speaking public for a writer. A third annotator ('pon my word 'tis so) of this same copy of *Cherry,* by her implied admiration for moral sentiments presumably a lady, was the most delightful of all. It is unfortunate that Mr. Sudgeberry did not know her; he would have made vastly more of a hit with her than he did with "Cherry," as wherever he becomes most offensively ponderous, and egotistical he most impressed her. This charming lady, evidently utterly mistaking the author's sly—too sly—humor for the earnest expression of his own deepest convictions, had underscored such of Mr. Sudgeberry's observations as, "I have often remarked that those who most emphatically impress upon others the necessity for promptitude are most apt themselves to be dilatory," and "Let it never be denied that true learning commands respect even among the most ribald minds: for I was listened to with the most flattering attention." The relish with which this lady, typical perhaps of many literal readers, followed the comedy may be gathered from her underlining Mr. Sudgeberry's smug reflection as to (as it appeared to him) the course of his amours in the heart of the fair Miss Gray: "Ah, how wonderfully, little by little, do the seeds of affection grow!"

In view of Mr. Tarkington's mature development it is curious indeed to contemplate the talent displayed in *Cherry*, the earliest written of his books. The talent is fine enough; the trouble with it precisely is that it is that fine kind which does not thrive in this stolid world. *Cherry* is a piece of virtuosity. There is about it an implication of the dilettante. Certainly it does not in the least reveal any capacity for reading the great public heart; Mr. Tarkington learned first how to write well, and then to be a professional writer, one of the most practical and expert now going. And it would be hard to find in this bouquet any foreshadowing of the robust intellectual energy of the study of character in *The Flirt*, or of the pounding satire of *The Turmoil*, or anything of the temper, the startling ferocity, of the book which in order of publication immediately followed it.

Freakish kind of thing altogether, probably difficult to match in the story of publishing, that *Cherry* should have been followed by such a book by the same hand as *In the Arena*.

* * * * *

An earlier commentator remarks that Mr. Tarkington "has an imperishable faith in the innate goodness of the human heart," and this (now legendary) imperishable faith of his, it has often in effect been intimated, "gives to the people of his fancy a certain whole-souled quality that makes them lovable even while we feel that they are a little bit too good to be true." Immortal writers have been turned from relentless naturalism, and been betrayed, by a generous heart. The infinite tenderness of Fielding was mightier, in *Amelia*, than the logic of art. The strong vein of kindly sentiment in Mr. Tarkington, throughout his work, his most ardent admirer could not deny. And the pervasion of much of his work by an excess of this quality has, indeed, obscured the possibility of considering him as a "novelist of ideas." In any consideration of his development, Mr. Tarkington's next book, passed over by some with brief mention as "in no way distinctive," demands (looking back from the present) very much more attention than has been given it by any critic. One thing about it which even at the time of its publication should have caused one to be knocked over by a feather is that there are no "heroes" in any of the six stories in it, unless we except the last.

For a year or two after writing *The Two Vanrevels* Mr. Tarkington's activities were attracted to the political field, and by taking a seat in the Indiana legislature he performed what many of his admirers have regarded as one of the great *im*practical jokes of his life. The political campaigning into which he plunged with boyish zest was a "find" for the newspaper paragraphers of the day. The "actor-acrobat" joke, the gorgeous waistcoat story, the "doughnut story," the tale of electioneering in a piano factory, and all the other joyous yarns, now hoary bromidioms, it is well to leave in the limbo which shelters them. Mr. Tarkington's political speeches were declared to have been a keen delight to his intimates. After his first speech, it has been said, the committee gathered about him with such encouraging expressions as, "Well, you tried, anyway." At any rate, it seems quite clear that the college orator was not a Hector in politics: our old friend Mr. "John-a-Dreams" relates that the literary candidate addressed a gathering of colored citizens in a colored church, and after he had talked four minutes two brethren were sound asleep. He is said to have admitted to a friend that perhaps he was a little impractical in going to Irish and "South-Side" gatherings in his automobile. It is pertinent here to note that in this much of a glimpse of him in his campaigning he appears, as in his writings, a remarkably democratic aristocrat; on one side a patrician of the Mr. Galsworthy pattern, and, on the other, as much of a "good mixer," with his ear just as close to the ground, as his onetime political colleague, Samuel Lewis Shank (likewise not unknown to fame), auctioneer, erstwhile Mayor of Indianapolis, pioneer advocate of municipal markets, and, later, vaudeville performer.

If Mr. Tarkington was a "kid glove candidate," he seems (by his political testament) to have been one that, like his *Boss Gorgett*, played the game as he found it; and his familiarity with the details of the campaign of which he was a part, one admirer has euphuistically said, included a knowledge of "what ever' nigger got." Mr. Tarkington was elected as a Republican, but soon became an insurgent. The two points of his career as a law-maker which I myself recall were his motion, shortly after his arrival in the legislative body, to have the time of meeting changed to one hour later in the morning, and his defense, against strong opposition by an ultra "respectable" class, of a bill providing for Sunday base-ball. Mr. Tarkington's prime services as a statesman, and they cannot be said to be mild, were rendered obliquely, in the way of criticism. His reaction to practical politics, of course, was a reaction very natural in a highly-keyed young man suddenly confronted, probably for the first time, with an array of the ugly and sordid facts of life; and it brought forth in him qualities heretofore latent, and totally unsuspected, and into which he has grown into-most power.

Critics have had Mr. Tarkington fixed as a romanticist, and critics have had him fixed as a realist; but the gods privily had it fixed that he was to be something more uncommon. The author of *In the Arena* would change manners; he would portray them, that men by seeing them would learn their evil or ridiculousness—in short, he definitely revealed himself as a satirist—a chafer under existing conditions,—a critic. June, and wine, and roses, and belletristic grace, and the he's-a-jolly-good-fellow-Glee-Club air have suddenly quite gone by the board in *In the Arena*, and in their stead appears an apparition wonderful to see over Mr. Tarkington's way, a Carlylesque indignation and vehemence. The Mr. Tarkington of *In the Arena* is the Mr. Tarkington heading toward the Mr. Tarkington of *The Turmoil*. There is a good deal of the same fiery energy, the same kind of rip-roaring earnestness, the same moral intensity in the sharp, smashing style, the same *mordant* wit. Mr. Brownell says of Lowell's wit that Lowell possessed too little *malice* to be distinctly penetrating. And in this stinging quality, which entered into Mr. Tarkington's wit in his political sketches, he is distinguished to-day beyond any American writer of fiction that I can think of.

When the fruits of Mr. Tarkington's political observation were appearing in magazine publication, I have heard, Mr. Roosevelt, then President, sent for the author to come to Washington, and throughout luncheon, before a number of other guests, scolded him for putting forth matter which Mr. Roosevelt felt had a tendency "to keep decent men out of politics"; though when the book was published, I understand, Mr. Roosevelt admitted that it was "good stuff." Mr. Tarkington himself sets considerable store by *In the Arena;* it is the only early book of his, the only one before *Beauty and the Jacobin*, which, he affirms, he "could stand to re-read." The reviewers who felt that "the author's estimate of the situation was a pretty true one" were right enough, as, even in the most startling instances, the basis of his material, he acknowledges, was fact. The ghastly story, "The Aliens," in which a gang of Italians who could not be trusted to vote crooked were infected with smallpox by the policy ticket device of a ward politician was built upon an idea which the author encountered revolving in the brain of a perfectly live politician.

In the Arena has this peculiarity: a number of the reviewers spoke of the "wide divergence of merit" of the stories it contains; and each selected a favorite of his own as the best. The five stories which deal with the psychology of politics, while the underlying attitude of the author—that of the cynical humorist—is the same in all, exhibit a wide divergence in character, display a talent of various notes. "Mrs. Protheroe," the story of a ravishing lady lobbyist of infinite resource and sagacity, whose wiles and fascinations exerted in the interest of renting her base-ball ground on Sunday, were the undoing of Senator Alonzo Rawson from Stackpole, "chairman, ma'am, of the Committee on drains and dikes," a raw-boned, half-educated, confident and intensely earnest young man, "who had, by years of endeavor, succeeded in moulding his features to present an aspect of stern and thoughtful majesty whenever he 'spoke,'" and who nightly addressed his Maker (in the loud voice of one accustomed to talking across wide out-of-door spaces) for guidance,—this is a story in which the author reflects his perception of a sordid truth by means of a highly finished kind of farce. While "The Aliens," in which the happy, tender love of Pietro Tobigli, that gay young chestnut vender, he of the radiant smiles, and

Bertha, rosy waitress in the little German restaurant, meets destruction by the hideous schemes, for "votin' seven Dagoes," of Mr. Frank Pixley, Republican precinct committee-man, "a pock-marked, damp-looking, soiled little fungus of a man," who "had attained to his office because, in the dirtiest precinct of the wickedest ward in the city, he had, through the operation of a befitting ingenuity, forced a recognition of his leadership,"—this is an exercise in "grimness" which, coming from the Mr. Tarkington of that time, is well-nigh terrific. The Zolaesque Mr. Tarkington certainly did a very thorough job of it in "The Aliens"; he had several chances, on the way, to lighten the blackness of his ending; but, having put his hand to this particular plow, he would not turn aside from the worst.

In turning over in one's mind the stories of this volume one is fairly staggered by the Schopenhauer-like pessimism which is the upshot of the whole thing. In every case, save one, the tragic failure results directly from a very earnest desire on the part of someone to do "right." It is the over-zealous reforming impulse of the theoretical politician, Farwell Knowles, editorial writer on the *Herald*, which throws him; it is Toby Tobigli's unshakable belief in the holiness of the Republican cause which is his death; Uncle Billy Rollison, whose reputation for honesty is the apple of his eye, is undone by his love for his son; Senator Rawson is persuaded to disaster by his simple belief that great beauty is great goodness; and Melville Bickner kills himself by unselfish labor. Mr. Tarkington's extraordinary burst of pessimism, however, is of a peculiar warm-hearted kind. It is quite without the cold cynicism of the man detached from his species who merely notes how destinies are controlled by a push in the dark. And it is equally devoid of the contempt for the lowly expressed in, for instance, such a pessimistic novel as George Moore's *Esther Waters*. While in "The Aliens" the author perceives, with revolt at the fact, the futility of virtue, as ever he sees and cherishes the virtue itself as a thing bright and beautiful. And his tragedy gets its poignancy from its striking contrast with the interwoven tenderness and humor. The author's "imperishable" compassion for the frailties of human nature finds an excellent vehicle of expression in "The Need of Money"—the story of how it happened, through the cruel machinations of politics, that Uncle Billy Rollison, a life-long Democrat and "a man as honest as the day is long," who far back in his corner sat through the dragging routine of the legislative session wondering what most of it meant, voted, because of the difficulties of his son Henry, to kill a party measure and was in consequence "read out of his party."

Mr. Tarkington's new-found gift, however, his

malice, perhaps bites deepest in "Hector"; that ringing, stinging sketch of a certain kind of temperament which goes very far in politics thanks to its sheer egoism disguised by a talent for moral platitudes. "Hector" is a companion picture to *The Flirt*. In *In the Arena* the writer of exceedingly popular though artistically somewhat wobbly-constructed novels made his debut as a "crack" technician in the short story form according to the canons of the treatises. And *In the Arena*, for all its force and feeling, is notable among Mr. Tarkington's early realistic books for his grasp of the literary virtue of restraint.

* * * * *

One of the outstanding popular successes of its season in 1905 was *The Conquest of Canaan*. The reviewers, beguiled perhaps by the magnetic figure of the author, amiably agreed in general that the book deserved all the prosperity it enjoyed. Mr. Tarkington himself to-day doesn't like the book, he says; and the "face" he makes at mention of it certainly indicates a strong distaste. Judge Pike he denounces as "bad." He was "introduced for the sake of the plot—one shouldn't have a plot—it's ruinous—a story should grow out of its characters." Such is the artistic creed of the present past master of plot novels. Or, if Mr. Tarkington was never a "master" of the plot (and, as we see, his gift was always for better things), for long the lure of the plot mastered him.

That *The Conquest of Canaan* is a grand hurrah of "melodrama," no one can be tempted to dispute; though it is a kind of melodrama which Mr. Tarkington made peculiarly a fine art of his own in fiction: the "refined melodrama" of *Broadway*, not the coarse and vulgar brand of Third Avenue and the historic old *Bowery*. Men of literary genius can be found who were not frightened of melodrama. What else, except literature, is *Treasure Island?* And the designation, melodrama, no longer bears the slurring connotation it once did. Some distinguished exponents and critics of the stage have gone on record as asserting that in the near future all drama will be melodrama. The word, in fact, has acquired a definite respectability, though, indeed, its precise significance be remarkably vague. Melodrama, we know, once meant a play with songs interspersed.

The Conquest of Canaan, at any rate, is distinctly a drama of situation, of environment on the one hand and of plot on the other. Though no one could say that there is not real character—that there are not real characters—in the book. The trouble with the plot is that it is such a cheap one. And the trouble with the characters is that by far the most telling ones, simply as characters, are quite subordinate and unessential, merely a part of the very colorful local color.

> Brekeke-kesh, koash, koash,
> Shall the Choral Quiristers of the Marsh
> Be censured and rejected as hoarse and harsh;
> And their Chromatic essays
> Deprived of praise?

Mr. Tarkington's great stroke of pure art in *The Conquest of Canaan* is his chorus of the Aristophanic comedy, which, comically enough, is far the best, the purest, of his comedy. Even the harshest critic of the book, Mr. Tarkington himself, admits that they are lovely: they of "the Forum," the conclave at the wide windows, or who in summer held against all comers the cane-seated chairs before the "National House" (which commanded the gates of the city), the wise men, the aged men, the hoary men, the town fathers, the sages, the patriarchs, the brethren, whose breath was "argument"; and whose very names are a joy—Eskew Arp, Colonel Flitcroft, Squire Buckalew, and the rest.

The humorously sardonic Mr. Arp, obsessed by his malevolent conception of "an ornery world-full," yet whose heart deep down is as soft as that of My Uncle Toby, is a not altogether unworthy—distant—cousin to that sublime company of crack-brains forever celebrated by "poor Yorick" in *Tristram*

Shandy. And Eskew's last "argument" to the conclave seems like some tender travesty of Colonel Newcome's *adsum* in the presence of his Master.

The first chapter of *The Conquest of Canaan* strongly suggests the delightful realistic comedy of Mr. Howells; and in its more sober moments throughout the book reminds one of Mr. Howells' *genre* pictures. For in its stage setting, *The Conquest of Canaan* is, like *The Gentleman from Indiana* (though perhaps more shrewd and zestful in this), a realistic study of manners in a typical American town, an authentic human document, and so on. The author's unrestrained exuberance of spirits in creative fancy and his close observation in detailed description are curiously interwoven. One of the most fantastic scenes in the story, for instance, one where the author's Gargantuan humor, like joy at *Beaver Beach,* reigns literally unconfined, the Sunday procession of Joe and Ariel, which threatens with "petrifaction" the "church-comers," is set in an Anthony-Trollope-like (or perhaps, in its sprightliness, a Jane-Austen-like) picture of the rites of the Canaanite Sabbath. The setting of *The Conquest of Canaan*, indeed, has everywhere the ring of complete fidelity.

There are several things about this early story which take on an interest peculiar to a study of the author's whole work. We get, for one thing, the first whiff of the later coming into full flower of Mr. Tarkington's literally world-famous juvenile society. The tall gentleman in his nineteenth year, Mr. *Bantry*, familiarly known to the conclave as Fanny Louden's boy, wearer of strange and brilliant garments, suggestive to the Forum of a "patent-medicine troupe," smoker of (what Mr. Arp called) the "cigareet," he of the yellow banjo case, the bone-handled walking-stick, and the man-of-the-world gait new at that time to Canaan,—Mr. Bantry may now be viewed as a prophetic figure, harbinger of William Baxter. He, however, like everybody else in *The Conquest of Canaan*, straightway falls rather violently into the plot, and ceases to be quite human, shortly after his triumphal return from college to the humble town which he had honored with his birth. His vivid early presence, however, indicates that what might be called the Young Adam was always strong in this author.

Another figure in *The Conquest of Canaan* fraught with tidings of future characters of greatness is Spec, as he was called for short, Respectability, his full name, Joe Louden's yellow dog. It is instructive to note the character of Spec, to remark his kinship with Duke, lowly confrère of Penrod, and, too, with Clematis, property of Genesis in *Seventeen*. Spec was "a small, worn, light-brown scrub-brush of a dog, so cosmopolitan in ancestry that his species was as undeterminable as the cast-iron dogs of the Pike Mansion." And these dogs of the Pike Mansion, which were honored by coats of black paint and shellac, "were of no distinguishable species or breed, yet they were unmistakably dogs; the dullest must have recognized them as such at a glance, which was, perhaps, enough." Spec, too, was a victim of the inexorable plot of *The Conquest of Canaan*, with most disastrous consequences to his bodily structure. It is very interesting, too, to observe that Spec's function, as the innocent object of surcharged wrath which must find some outlet, is the same as that of that "lami*dal*" Moor in *The Turmoil*.

Again in *The Conquest of Canaan* Mr. Tarkington is the moralist. Though some reviewers read a strange "lesson" into the book: that it taught that all respectable people are narrow-minded and dishonest, and that all the really desirable virtues are to be found in the dissolute and disruptable. The theme of the story, briefly stated, is simply the difficulty (in this Puritanically Canaan-like world) of living down a bad reputation after it has once been firmly established. Joe, the scalawag of Canaan, an outcast (as Mr. Arp put it) "as black as a preacher's shoes on Sunday," is—a pronounced instance of Mr. Tarkington's cherished type, the character in maladjustment with his environment—seen with a more intelligent and understanding eye than that of

Canaan. Mr. Tarkington is always all for the under dog. And by means of Joe's sympathy with the society into which he is thrust, the riffraff of the riffraff, the "boys and girls" (as the fatherly manager of that establishment called them) of the disruptable *Beaver Beach*, the author exercises what, in works more seriously regarded, some critics speak of as a "Russian compassion." Such parts of Mr. Tarkington's story as constitute a brief for the despised of the world clearly escape (what "Russian compassion" does not always do) sentimentality; and are written with manly good humor, strength and dignity. Though perhaps, as style, they are a bit too eloquent.

A figure very significant too in the light of the later workings of Mr. Tarkington's mind is the low-life lady of Canaan, the tawdry and rouged Claudine, who so hated "to have gen'lemen quarrelling" over her, especially her husband, Mr. Fear. The character of Mrs. Fear is perceived with something considerably more than, as first appears, the eye of the rollicking humorist. The story's hero, heroine and villain are at bottom the old familiar trio of melodrama; and it is in keeping that their typical qualities should be superlative. As serious fiction the story falls down, of course, in that the thrilling situations in which it abounds involve coincidences that strain the reader's imagination, and that hardly one of these situations grows naturally and logically out of the characters involved. The tragedy which Mrs. Fear precipitates, however, is quite the psychological result of the Mrs. Fear nature, and the symptoms of the malady which is Claudine's character are recorded by a Mr. Tarkington curiously omitted from the Tarkington legend. Mr. Tarkington's recognition of the fact of Mrs. Fear's being in the world repeats a bit of the pessimism of *In the Arena*. But there is a point that concerns us a little more than that in this little sketch of a sinister nature. The touch of the scientist in the blend of things in Mr. Tarkington's mature equipment has had conspicuously little recognition. Claudine is the earliest expression of Mr. Tarkington's increasing tendency to pathological interest in the type of the dangerous woman.

There is another scientific touch to *The Conquest of Canaan* which is very curious indeed, and very expressive of the soundness of Mr. Tarkington's methods as an artist, when not betrayed by the germ of melodrama in his blood. This is the author's building a love scene of much charm, which rises even to heights of poetic feeling, the tryst of Joe and Ariel "across the Main Street bridge at noon," upon the phenomenon which students of alcoholism term disassociation of personality. Mr. Tarkington's first drunkard, Mr. Wilkerson, moving about the stage like Mrs. Gamp, was perhaps a bit on the order of the humorous stage drunkard. But never in any other instances are Mr. Tarkington's drunkards figures in whom intoxication is merely artistically effective for the occasion; they are nervous cases; the roots of their condition may be discerned extending back into the circumstances of their lives. They are all, Mr. Fisbee, Joe Lane, Joe Louden, Crailey Gray, Larrabee Harman, Uncle Billy Rollinson, Ray Vilas, Roscoe Sheridan, well understood alcoholics, each representative of one of the many varieties of the temperament.

Perhaps the truest and cleverest bit of writing in *The Conquest of Canaan* is a scene which is an earnest of Mr. Tarkington's peculiar power, later so happily cultivated, of depicting the social tortures suffered by the adolescent: the scene of the last dancing party to which Ariel goes, before (in good, old melodramatic fashion) she "falls heiress" and goes to Paris to "learn to dress"; and this chapter of utter frustration and humiliation is a fine and tender touch.

From a point shortly after the former hoyden, and "outsider," Ariel returns from Europe a vision of loveliness and fashion and "all cultured up," as Eskew put it, to wreck havoc with the male population of Canaan, and when Joe takes up his fight against the great boog-a-boo, Judge Pike, Canaan's millionaire and dictator, the story becomes melodrama frank and unashamed; and has the interest for this study of exhibiting Mr. Tarkington at his most purple. As to Judge Pike himself, with his big, splotched, Henry-the-Eighth face and his bull-bass voice, as one critic put it, "when he was bad, he was very, very bad, and when he was good he was horrid." When he taunts the virtuous heroine with the loss of her gold you can fairly hear the hisses from the gallery. Mr. Fear's telling lawyer Joe not to worry about "gittin' law practice," that if there's no other way some of the "boys" will go out and make some "fer" him, is a stroke to bring down the house. The scene in which Joe confronts Judge Pike with his villainies is enough to send shivers down the spine of any reader not hopelessly "cultured up." And the "curtain," with Joe roaringly acclaimed idol of the populace, and Mayor-elect of Canaan, is quite the "great Harkless" "stunt" over again.

The author lays it on with a dripping brush. And there can be no doubt that there is uncommon skill, and even power, in the way he does it. The defect is not in ability, but is one of taste. The "whole show" which the author has hit upon has an amusingly human quality, too, in that Joe's spectacular career is the "pipe dream," with himself in the role of hero, of every wastrel born; and so, doubtless, in some form or other, is in the thoughts of all those whose thoughts are the long, long thoughts of youth.

In places in *The Conquest of Canaan* the resemblance to real life, one must say, is pretty faint; yet here, too, as in all of Mr. Tarkington's work, the effect is that somehow we do seem to be tasting life even when our credulity is most overtaxed. As a "ripper" *The Conquest of Canaan* is, being more consistent, a more crafty artistic success than *The Gentleman from Indiana*, but it lacks the youthful sincerity, the richness of imaginative inspiration, the *flair*, of the earlier book. All in all, it pointed away from the light.

VI

IN turning over the reviews of Mr. Tarkington's books, the notices contemporary with their publication, one's interest is engaged by the number of times the word "trifle" is applied as a term of designation. The term is invariably employed by these reviewers in a sympathetic sense, and it may be embraced as a happy one for its purpose. Its repetition, too, is suggestive of a critical fancy. In Mr. Tarkington's hands, the trifle—the short piece, light as air, and irradiant with color—becomes a distinct literary form (as the sonnet is a distinct form, or the essay). Mr. Tarkington's *forte* for these delicate morsels of unexpected flavor reminds one of nothing so much as Whistler's genius for debonair, exquisite, and inimitable little drawings in colored chalks. They, too, were trifles, and they were perfection. If the soul of Whistler were to come back among us as that of a writer, I think this author would write something very much in the form of *Monsieur Beaucaire*, or of *Cherry*, or (most likely of all) *The Beautiful Lady*.

It may also be remarked that the sum of the world's literature of perfect trifles is not very large. Any collection of such pieces—were one to be made, like the volumes of the World's Greatest Short-Stories—would have to give a good place to *The Beautiful Lady*. The very fetching opening of this very charming bagatelle—the discovery of the youthful and impoverished Neapolitan gentleman, his humiliated, shaven pate adorned in brilliant letters with the legend: *Théâtre Folie-Rouge Revue de Printemps Tous les Soirs!* and seated at a small table under an awning at "the centre of the inhabited world" (before the Café de la Paix at the corner of the Place de l'Opéra), the butt of an amused throng—suggests somewhat the bright air of the *New Arabian Nights*, and particularly the idea of the adventures of the young man with the cream tarts. The sparkling and whimsical beginning, this, of a delicately wrought idyl, the peculiar and illusive flavor of which is due in no small measure to the skill with which the author makes the very engaging Neapolitan tell the story in a variety of English which he flatters himself is triumphantly idiomatic, but which at times is fearfully and wonderfully constructed.

There is a suggestion of Stevenson, too, in the high polish of this curious style, in the niceties of the Neapolitan's language, which has something of a mincing step. Like himself, Ansolini's language is wonderfully "fine in the coat." And the lightly sketched villain, the fortune-hunting Prince Caravacioli,—monocle, handsome nose, toupée, yellow skin, dyed-black moustache, splendid height—is quite of the Stevenson type. The wild and kind-hearted young "North American nobleman," however, Lambert R. Poor, Jr., who desired to "create considerable trouble for Paris," and whose slang and deportment so mystify the sober-minded Ansolini, is pure Tarkington. In the chapters in which the Neapolitan endeavors vainly to dissuade his charge from his announced purpose concerning Paris, and in the piquant contrast between the two young men—both gentlemen—there is humor of a very distinguished order—humor of a quality which is to be found in few books.

The glamorous Lady herself, the sense of a beautiful presence, is conveyed with something of the subtle touch of the author of *The Portrait of a Lady*. One of the achievements of *The Beautiful Lady*, however, is that it is a very happy portrait of a gentleman, a man of gentle birth and feeling,—Ansolini. The gentle, playful humor which pervades the story has a peculiarly fragrant quality. Quaintly droll is Ansolini's touching study of feet, pantaloons, and skirts. There is just enough criticism of life to give a desirable effect of body to the airy tale. And this is most ingeniously done, as it is through the eyes of Ansolini that one sees a group of "those strange beings of the Western republic, at whom we are perhaps too prone to pass from one of ourselves to another the secret smile, because of some little imperfections of manner." If the characters of the story are hardly more than sketched in, they are distinctly, deliciously realized; and all of them is given that is essential to the play of the story.

As is frequently the case with Mr. Tarkington, and quite as it should be with a "trifle," the story you are told is no story at all, or rather, if stated in the terms of a synopsis, a very foolish one; but you have been treated to a great deal of charm. Perhaps it is because of this reason, that the story is mainly a succession of little touches, that one likes it better after a second reading than at the first, and still better after the third. Try it. One hostile critic of *The Beautiful Lady* has been found, who remarked of the theme that "a French writer alone could have done it,"—let us add, better, or even, as well. *The Beautiful Lady*, lacking the dramatic action of *Beaucaire*, equals it in its pathos, and surpasses it in the originality of its conception and in its whimsically tender humor.

The autobiographical trail throughout Mr. Tarkington's work sometimes comes to light in unexpected places. Among his escapades, Poor, Jr., you remember, dragged his "governess" with him to make the balloon ascent at the Porte Maillot "on a windy evening." With uproarious gusto Mr. Tarkington, in a letter to his nephews, written from Paris in

1904, describes a balloon ascension there made by, so he signs himself, their "exalted Uncle." This letter concludes thus:

> Well, I know you envy me now as much as you admire me. Think of having an Uncle who has been up in a real balloon! It isn't every boy that has that kind of an Uncle. Next time I go up (and I am going, because I have your interests at heart!) I want to take Papa John—but somehow I think we'll have to be diplomatic about it until we have come down safely. I would like to be the only relative of you that has ever been up in a balloon, yet I am willing to give you a Grandfather, too, who has been as great a help to you as your Uncle. I admit it is a great sacrifice, but I can see what a great benefit it will be to you to have not only an Uncle, but a Grandfather, in the balloon business. Still, for the present, you have an Uncle who has been up in a balloon—to say nothing of an Aunt who dropped a hat on the top of the Eiffel Tower.

Mr. Tarkington's discovery of Europe resulted in several "trifles." Some of these take on more interest in the light of a study of the whole, and the why and wherefore of his work, than they had simply as independent stories. One such in particular is *His Own People*, an absurdly elementary sort of story, very well *written*. As a story, that is, as a plot and its development, one's first impression is that this tale is (so to say) so beardless that it seems a shame to attack it. The critic has an embarrassed feeling that there is something ungentlemanly about such a course. Mr. Tarkington's assembling here of an altogether "bad lot" of Europeans of a very fashionable effect quite reminds one of the amusing collection of personages of this class in *What Maisie Knew.* Mr. James' types there, however, carry the conviction of being the real article, and Mr. Tarkington's characters here have somewhat the effect of wearing a theatrical make-up for their parts—false moustaches, and that sort of thing. And the bogus nature of their *distingué* character is altogether too bogus to fool anybody less simple than the altogether too simple Robert Russ Mellin, of Cranston, Ohio, U. S. A. At least, that is the effect on the reader, though there is an intimation in the story that nobody could come up to the Robert Russ Mellin type in the Grand Central Station and sell him such a gold-brick as he would "fall for" in the fairy-land atmosphere of the Europe which he visits. And the transparent nature of this particular lot of crooks may be an intentional stroke of the author's, one of the points, in his mind, of the story. The figures of this unsavory group, perhaps, are designed as samples of a very populous class which infested the Europe of the time: they are so patently bogus in the picture, he might say, because that is the way they *are*.

Though there is, even to the reader who is not in young Mr. Mellin's shoes, a bit of glamour about the villainess, the enchantress Hélené,—a slow-music type which apparently Mr. Tarkington was much taken with artistically, as she appears again (or a reincarnation of her), under the same name even, in *The Man from Home*. The grotesque Honorable Chandler Pedlow, supposedly of the "North American Chamber of Deputies," is done with all the exaggerated emphasis of the old time *Bowery* boards. But the author comes back again to very shrewdly perceived realism in his intellectually diverting sketch of the low-class Londoner, Sneyd, the wonderful English of whose type is quite equalled by Mr. Tarkington's mimicry of it. One of the main points of the little story, however,—from the point of view of critical study—is the homespun (and thoroughly Tarkingtonian) moral, which the author not only draws, but tells right out, and at considerable length. This Sunday-school lesson is that you are to appreciate the genuine, wholesome things back home in "the States," which are finer than all the glamorous foreign geegaws,—a little moral which recalls the conviction of Senator Rawson, in *In the Arena*, when he suspected that the fashionable Mrs. Protheroe would not after all come to meet him, that "the Stackpole girls were nobler by far at heart than many who might wear a king's-ransom's worth of jewels round their throats at the opera-house in a large city."

This (whether or not it is a "true story") juvenile and lurid story gets the high class quality which it has altogether from the excellence of the writing. The altogether charming opening, the picture of the glass-domed palm-room of the Grand Continental Hotel Magnifique in Rome, is very much in Mr. James' most agreeable manner. Remarkably suggestive of the delicate impressions of that cultivated gentleman is the fancy at play in the description of this place of "vasty heights and distances, filled with a mellow green light which filters down languidly through the upper foliage of tall palms, so that the two hundred people who may be refreshing or displaying themselves there at the tea-hour have something the look of under-water creatures playing, upon the sea-bed." And, a bit later in young Mr. Mellin's reverie, that "dozen men and women, dressed for dinner, with *a goldfish officer or two* among them, who swam leisurely through the aquarium on their way to the hotel restaurant" is much like one of Mr. James' graceful literary amenities. Further, the young Mr. Mellin even seems to be a sort of male counterpart to the onetime very celebrated Daisy Miller, in whose existence a sharp rebuke was aimed at American girls who travelled abroad. The fatuous complacence of Mr. Mellin's early savoring of the "superiority" of the old Europe, his puerile intoxication with his idea of the "beau monde," with the "artificial odors," and the "sumptuousness" of "the finest essence of Old World society mingling in Cosmopolis," is a carefully traced criticism of one aspect of Mr. Tarkington's own people.

That passionately provincial American, Mr. Nicholson, lays much stress on the "cosmopolitan" aspect of Mr. Tarkington as an Indiana writer. It is probable that Mr. Tarkington's continual cavorting about between various points in the United States (Kennebunkport, Maine,—New York City,—Princeton, New Jersey,—Chicago,—and Indianapolis) has a cosmopolitan air to such home-keeping hearts as Mr. Nicholson's. But Mr. Tarkington,—for all his residence for a span in France and Italy, for all his enthusiasm for the Island of Capri, where for a period he made his home, and despite the fact that during his sojourn in France he became acclimated to a degree that he was (as I have heard it put) "one of the craziest Frenchmen of the whole lot,"—has never, in the remotest, been a cosmopolite in the sense that, say, Mr. James was; of whom it was one time said, with perhaps some asperity, that he "was at home in every country but his own." Again and again and again, in Mr. Tarkington's books it is asked of the globe-trotter in the Hoosier land if he does not find the atmosphere here dull, "provincial," "unsympathetic"? And his answer to this question is designed to go a long way in showing him up either as a decent fellow or a cad. Joe Louden finds Canaan "bully"; Valentine Corliss is decidedly superior to Capitol City. And if it cannot be said that Mr. Tarkington abroad was at heart himself decidedly the man from "home" (and doubtless such an observation would wing its way to where it would appear pretty *bizarre*), in his work we find him abroad in humorous sympathy, at least, with the crassest of his fellow countrymen.

Daniel Voorhees Pike, attorney at law, Kokomo, Indiana, the "Man from Home," is a humorist-critic of Old World society quite back in the vein of *The Innocents Abroad*, and doubtless would weep with Mark Twain over the grave of Adam. In his boisterous ridicule of various traditional Continental ideas he is very much in the spirit of *Martin Chuzzlewit* reversed. Mr. Pike would "not trade the State Insane Asylum at home for the worst ruined ruin in Europe." But the joke is not altogether on Mr. Pike; he is a sort of American Don Quixote, beautiful in his grotesqueness. While the authors of the play, Mr. Tarkington in collaboration with Harry Leon Wilson, banter him with hilarious joy in his outlook, they also respect his genuineness and hard-headed worth. The prodigious joke of the play, indeed, has been on the American theatre audience. Whenever, with, of course, humorous intention, Mr. Pike is made to make the eagle scream most vociferously, these very screams have evoked volumes of applause in earnest approval of the sentiments expressed. "Yes, ma'am!" says Mr. Pike, "there's just as many kinds of people in Kokomo as there is in Pekin." "Hurrah! Right-O!" has come from the throats of innumerable spiritual brothers and sisters of Mr. Pike in the house. So this frolic conceived in a spirit of good natured satire has had the curiously misdirected reward of, almost, one continuous succession of wonderfully successful gallery-plays. Ethel is enraged at Mr. Pike's audacity in prying into the affairs of the Earl of Hawcastle to learn what is thought of him by "the best citizens." "Why, I'd 'a done that," says Mr. Pike, "if it had been the Governor of Indiana himself!" (Loud applause.) *The Man from Home*, as a "spectacular conglomeration" (as the circus posters say) of such "heart throbs" (as they have proved to be) as this, is certainly a remarkable production.

This play of joint authorship exhibits in what might be called an undraped way many of Mr. Tarkington's principal foibles as a constructor of plots. Here, as, in a measure, in many of his stories, we have a situation depending on the meretricious device of a series of misunderstandings and mistaken identities. Behold: quite at the right moment the supposedly simple German traveller, affably addressed by the Kokomoian as "Doc," turns out to be the powerful Grand-Duke Vasili Vasilivitch (even as *Beaucaire* stood revealed a prince of the royal blood); zip! an escaped anarchist is whisked into the disguise of a chauffeur; a whole company of tricksters, male and female (little better, as Mr. Pike intimated, than a lot of Terre Hut pickpockets), pass themselves off as the flower of European aristocracy; and the Man from Home himself, in reality the brightest, shrewdest, most forceful personality of the whole lot, voluntarily poses as a very simple, ingenuous personality. All this is clearly brought forward by Mr. Frederick Taber Cooper in his careful, brief study of Mr. Tarkington, published a number of years ago in his *Some American Story Tellers*, or perhaps it is better to say, his study of the Mr. Tarkington of a number of years ago.

And the authors of the play lean very heavily indeed upon one of Mr. Tarkington's favorite trumps as a romanticist: coincidence. Mr. Cooper, who concerns himself almost altogether with the structure of this play, rides very hard the fact that everything happens in the nick of time: "a person is named, and miraculously he appears upon the scene; a secret is breathed, and somewhere a window or door opens stealthily and the secret is captured. A tangle of situations is tightly knotted up and the only people who can unravel it are supposedly scattered widely throughout Europe and Asia,—and presto! they are all discovered simultaneously beneath the roof of a Sicilian hotel." Time worn, and time honored, stage tricks, all. The note of "glorified melodrama" in all this amusing kind of thing of course cannot be denied. But that note, it is becoming more and more plain, most certainly is not, as this critic then found, "the essence of Booth Tarkington."

But what else, it may be asked with some reason, is there to *The Man from Home* besides glorified melodrama? Certainly the characters, though animated enough, are,—from Mr. Pike, on through,— the veriest manikins. The young Englishman, suitor for the hand (and settlement) of Miss Ethel Granger-Simpson, is just about as much of a wooden-Indian-on-wheels figure, as an Englishman, as the immemorial comic Irishman of the vaudeville stage is an authentic Irishman. And the sport made by Mr. Pike of ancestors, ruins, settlements, and so on, is regular American barber-shop humor, name-blown-in-the-bottle brand. Just so.

It is what might be called the "philosophy" of the play which is the meat of the nut for the student of the soul of Mr. Tarkington. The melodrama of it is incidental. If the authors of his being did not design the rampant provincialism of Mr. Pike as a trumpet call to the plain American citizen, and were making game of this a bit, in fact, at bottom they were altogether *with* Mr. Pike at his shrewdest. They were quite with Mr. Pike when he told his ward, Miss Simpson, that she was looking for something which there was nothing "to." They were heartily Kokomoian themselves in their disdain for the "Granger-Simpson" kind of affectation. And Mr. Tarkington, at least, cannot be accused of putting on for the occasion the home-grown, common philosophy of D. V. Pike. It is a point of view with which he has right along been in sympathy. It is the philosophy of Plattville. Tom Martin, for instance, who, in "Great Men's Sons," drew his own shrewd rustic moral from *L'Aiglon* after witnessing its production by Mme. Bernhardt and M. Coquelin at the "metropolis" of his state, commanded the trade in Dry Goods and Men's Clothing at Plattville. And though this slight but very effective sketch, *Great Men's Sons* (which has the effect of a verbatim report), first published in a magazine under the title of *The Old Grey Eagle*, is included in the collection of political stories, *In the Arena*, it does not logically so much belong there as it does, for purposes of comparative consideration, among what may be called Mr. Tarkington's foreign stories.

Great Men's Sons also gets its point,—the kind of point that Mr. Tarkington is fond of making in his foreign stories,—from the suggested contrast between the romantic glamour of thrones and titles and the simple pathos of actuality. The identical thing which as handled in *The Man from Home* is somewhat in the nature of slap-stick humor is very real and poignant in *Great Men's Sons*, where it has a kind of simple nobility. The violent comparison, made by Mr. Pike, in the play, of the ambition of Miss Granger (to ally herself with English "society") with little Annie Hoffmeyer (in *Great Men's Sons*), whose "pa" was a carpenter in Kokomo, and who couldn't get into the local Ladies' Literary Club, so got her "pa" to give her the money to marry Artie Seymour, the minister's son—this is exactly the effect of contrast wrought in the sketch where the character of "that ornery little cuss" L'Aiglon is compared, by the old pioneer, with the tale of silent self-sacrifice and splendid courage presented in the career of Orlando T. Bicker's boy: a young fellow with, as it is said, "the right kind of stuff in him" who fought an almost hopeless battle educating his sisters and younger brother, held the family together, kept his mother from want and won the love and respect of the whole community; and then, on the threshold of achievement, broke down from overwork and died as uncomplainingly as he had lived, without ever a thought that he had done anything more than his simple duty. It should be clear enough that Mr.

Tarkington, cosmopolite (if you will), aristocrat, collector of *objets d'art*, sincerely and greatly *admires* the homespun virtues. He is even naïve about it. And he is continually telling Sunday-school stories; what he had in mind in *Mister Antonio* (he one day let drop) was a Sunday-school story.

A touch further characteristic of the man who wrote *Great Men's Sons* (and *Cherry*) appears in the author's attitude toward the "high brow" "bounce" talked, in "a spikey little voice," by the character "Little Fiderson," "whose whole nervous person jerkily sparkled *L'Aiglon* enthusiasm." Was it not a notion of Dr. Johnson's that of all cant the worst was the "cant of criticism"? Doubtless the Tarkingtonian "horse-sense" of the great Cham of letters, if one may so put it, would have snorted, too, at Fiderson's: "I thought that after Wagram I could feel nothing more; emotion was exhausted; but then came that magnificent death! It was tragedy made ecstatic; pathos made into music; the grandeur of a gentle spirit, conquered physically but morally unconquerable! Goethe's 'More Light' outshone!"

But the doctor had considerable reverence, a kind of superstitious reverence maybe, for learning. And it is one of Mr. Tarkington's peculiarities that he shies at any suggestion of the "lofty dome" kind of thing. Some time ago (I have heard) he was walking in a street of his midland city when he met an old school acquaintance, now a professor in an eastern university.

"Hello, Albert," said Mr. Tarkington.

"Hello, Booth," said the professor.

"Let me see, what is it you are doing now?" asked Mr. Tarkington. And then he added quickly: "Oh, yes, I remember now. You are doing the serious."

The Middle Western people are preeminently humorons, particularly those of the Southern strain from which Lincoln sprang. And "blue jeans" philosophy, it may not be without point to note, has ever been one of the staples of the Indiana literary crop. It permeates, of course, and is the tang and savor of, the works of "Benj. F. Johnson, of Boone," better known the world round by his real name of Riley.

> I ain't, ner don't p'tend to be
> Much posted on philosophy;
> But thare is times, when all alone,
> I work out idees of my own.

It is their native "horse-sense" which gives the "puneh" to the fables of George Ade. And the Hoosier relish for the shrewd, homespun point of view is so pronounced that the feature in the local press which corresponds to the humorous column of greater metropolitan papers takes the turn of homely philosophy. Abe Martin, the hypothetical Brown

County sage, whose sayings are reported daily by Mr. Kin Hubbard in the Indianapolis *News*, has been for years (though his existence is purely of the spirit) one of the best-known public figures of Indiana. His Plattville-like observations last night were: "We all make fun of a circus behind its back. Mrs. Tilford Moot's niece has three children—two goin' t' school an' one t' th' dentist's."

Next after *His Own People* Mr. Tarkington published another foreign story, a novel in length, but another trifle in the light charm of its atmosphere (though it is indeed a tragi-comedy), *The Guest of Quesnay*, first issued in 1908. Some of Mr. Tarkington's enthusiastic admirers pronounced this the best piece of fiction he had produced up to that time,— while from other of his friends a reverse verdict has come. So much, at least, as Mr. Cooper acknowledges certainly is true: it is "a very agreeable Summer idyl pervaded by the soft sunshine, the fragrance of flowers and the singing of birds." And of its setting this critic happily adds that it is one which altogether brings "a thrill of nostalgia for the highways and byways of rural France," of the France of yesterday, before the World War. *The Guest of Quesnay*, too, has its own contributions to make to a study of the development of Mr. Tarkington's talent.

In this story, for one thing, the philosophy is not

of the homely variety, but it is—what startled some reviewers at the time of its publication—metaphysical. And, as one commentator noted, one would as soon have expected to find metaphysics in a bird's song as in one of *Booth Tarkington's* stories. In one place *The Guest of Quesnay* was banteringly received as "*Booth* Tarkington's happy discovery of the scientific process of regeneration." And perhaps in this book the author did indeed make some happy discoveries,—discoveries of qualities of mind which later he cultivated to effect.

The underlying mystery of *The Guest of Quesnay* is so transparent at least as early in its progress as the fifth or sixth chapter that, as in a leisurely fashion the story plays out its course, the reader is put in mind of that pleasant situation in the drama where there are plainly visible to the audience the legs of a gentleman much sought by the sword of his stage enemy, who industriously pokes about in every place but the right one. Any reader with a tithe of a mind in his head would know at once that the romantically beautiful and innocent young man with the Monte Cristo hair and the "singularly singular" manner who comes to the out-of-the-world Normandy inn, was, by some strange metamorphosis, none other than the powdered Silenus first met as one of the sights of the boulevards. Neither would he be long in doubt that the reputed "American lady who married a French nobleman," Madame d'Armond, guest at the nearby château, was—unknown to him—the wife lost to this strange gentleman. Though the beguiling busy-body who recounts the tale of it all, being himself much mystified by the Sinbad-the-Sailor character of the circumstances, succeeds in surrounding his people and his events with a certain amount of verbal fog.

A thing which strongly attracts the interest in a survey of Mr. Tarkington's work from first to last is this author's facility for investing himself with a style happily suited to each particular occasion. He has never become set in any one manner; never, as so many writers do, after having achieved success in one manner, has he continued to exploit a field already won. Mr. Chesterton, for instance (Grand Young Man of England that he is), is forever the same—Mr. Chesterton, master journalist. With Mr. Tarkington, as ever with the incorrigible artist, each creative bout is a wholly new adventure. The manner, the style, of *The Guest of Quesnay* is peculiar among Mr. Tarkington's books. For one thing, it is not often that, as here, he tells his story in the first person. He objects to this method on the ground (I have heard him say) that it is "too easy."

Much of the charm of *The Guest of Quesnay* undoubtedly arises from the pretty, essayical character of its style: leisurely in method, descriptive, discursive, mildly witty, gently sentimental. It has altogether an amusingly George-William-Curtis effect. This style is deliciously indicative of the character of the middle-aged, amateurish and conservative-minded landscape painter who tells the story, and his character in the role of narrator is essential to the success of the whole effect. The author slyly simulates the style of a man who, though he writes very well, professes that he is not a trained writer. One especially pleasant instance of the musty-bachelor humor of the writer appears in his soliloquy about the contrast of his antiquated dress clothes with those of the sartorially unexceptionable other gentlemen at the dinner party at Quesnay: "clothes differing from the essential so vitally as did mine must have seemed immodest, little better than no clothes at all." Just a touch of Mr. Tarkington's inveterate admiration for sterling worth is given to the character of the narrator of the story, in whom an honest heart beat beneath a poor man's coat.

One of the things which mark *The Guest of Quesnay* as a novel beyond the ordinary is its striking pictorial quality; the Paris streets and pleasant byways of the so much loved French countryside are "seen" with a joyousness in the singing qualities of color which reminds one of French impressionist painting. The vivid and sumptuous opening scene, the pageant of the boulevard,—women prevalent over all the concourse; "fine women in fine clothes; rich women in fine clothes; poor women in fine clothes,"—brings to mind one of the urban canvases of Pissarro. The monstrous figure which rolls into this scene, the appalling wreck of dissipation, the infamous Larrabee Harman, with "the look of a half-poisoned Augustan borne down through the crowds from Palatine after supping with Caligula," has revolted some moral readers. And doubtless he was intended by the author to be revolting enough. For my own part, however, I felt only a child-like delight in the gorgeousness of his ruin. The author spared nothing to make of him a champion. And Harman is as rich in degradation as Long John Silver is in villainy. While his consort, in the spectacular white automobile, the savagely graceful, dyed, enamelled dancer, *la belle Mariana*, is, as a bit of cynical drawing, almost Degasesque. And this Mariana, though we do not see a great deal of her, is of a good deal of significance. She is of the evil sisterhood which has so curiously attracted this author's scalpel. The Spanish courtesan, Mariana, whose nature is observed with a scientific lens, is of the same human stock as Claudine, and as the flirt Cora Madison, and the green-eyed Sibyl Sheridan.

The Guest of Quesnay is distinguished, too, among later-day novels by its elfish relish for character. The "most henlike waiter in France," Amédée, babbler, scandal-mongering, with the soul-of-honor pose and the eloquent gestures, whose talents were indeed lost in the country, and his friend the gossiping gardener Jean Ferret, are conceptions of delicious comedy. "Truly, truly," as Amédée would say. It is pleasant to note, too, in this maître d'hôtel, as a child of Mr. Tarkington's brain, that (though we are led to believe he cannot) he is convinced that he can sing.

Among the most amusing, attractive, and real of all Mr. Tarkington's "females," as Fenimore Cooper used to term his women characters, must be counted the incorrigible damsel, the thistle-brained creature, the elfin young lady Anne Elliott, she of the same name as the young lady of a very different type in Miss Austen's *Persuasion;* she who had the "*infantile* father," and who had not had a "*syllable* of food" since dawn. Most of the women in Mr. Tarkington's earlier books, it must be admitted, are not so much actual women as the embodiment of romantic and chivalrous dreams of women: Lady Mary Carlisle, Miss Sylvia Gray, and Helen Sherwood are examples of figures which in lifelikeness merely suffice for the movement of the story. Though Mrs. Protheroe takes on something of the air of this world. Miss Elliott, however, though very lightly sketched, is more nearly, in the slang phrase, "all there" than is usual in the author's earlier books.

The author's humorous conception in his Professor Keredec of a mountain walking is carried out with engaging zest. And Mr. Tarkington always shines in depicting the rattish type. His fox-faced youth Oil Poicy—which translated out of the New York argot would be Mr. Earl Percy—has in an abundant measure this author's Dickensian gusto for the humorons in low life. In fact, a reflection which must have struck the attentive reader of Mr. Tarkington is that if, instead of being inclined toward the more wholesome type of American story, he cared to do the sordid-side-of-big-cities kind of thing, which appeals so strongly to some of the younger men, he might out-Gissing the Gissingest.

But the startling thing about this summer story is the author's flirtation there with ideas of some considerable profundity. Mr. Cooper, in his study, has the "born story teller" within Mr. Tarkington neatly "rescued" from the "would-be maker of purposeful and serious fiction." And, as one of the reviewers of *The Guest of Quesnay* noted, Mr. Tarkington's "psychological optimism," his method there of making a good man out of a bad man, is perhaps "almost as impractical as Christianity." Still Christianity has advocates of its points. And the ethical beauty of the idea Mr. Tarkington has employed can hardly be denied. If it is, perhaps, not a new idea; yet no (or very few) ideas are. The thing of moment is that, as a popular novelist, he was concerned with it, or indeed had dalliance with any such idea at all.

Persons whose pasts, like that of Larrabee Harman, *alias* Oliver Saffren, have been blotted out by some injury to the brain have been the theme of more novels than it would be of any profit to number. Mr. Cooper, however, finds in this story a fresh suggestion: that we are all of us hampered by our knowledge of the evil in the world at large and more specifically in ourselves; and that if upon reaching maturity some circumstances should obliterate all this, leaving our minds as virgin as in early childhood, and give us a chance to start over again, to ignore evil and learn only what is good, we might make of ourselves far nobler men and women than we were before. The author rests with this suggestion; he proves nothing, nor does he try. His story ends on the threshold of the new life, with Harman recovered for youth and beauty and goodness; whether he is a permanently reformed character, or whether he slowly but inevitably drifts back into his old evil ways—perhaps is beside the point.

Professor Keredec is an idealist believing in the immutable goodness of man's spirit; and his metaphysics are of the order which do not bother about what has gone by and what is to come. "*That* is not *alive*. It *is* not!" And a man who shakes off his sin is clean; he stands as pure as if he had never sinned. But though his emancipation can be so perfect, there is a law that he cannot escape from the result of all the bad and foolish things he has done, for every act, every breath you draw, is immortal, and each has a consequence that is never ending. Now, in considering Mr. Tarkington, a very interesting thing about this idea of the moral consequences of natural law is that the same idea, in a somewhat more elementary form of expression, occurred to another of the author's erring heroes, none other than Hedrick Madison, who knew that "a man might become great, rich, honoured, and have a large family, but his one soft sin would follow him, hunt him out, and pull him down at last."

It was a bit before *The Guest of Quesnay* appeared that Mr. Maurice in his article in *The Bookman* suggested that it was perhaps odd that Mr. Tarkington, having so many of his intimates among writers, actors, and painters, had never taken one such character as the theme of a book; and Mr. Maurice concluded that maybe it was because such a study was not adapted to the nature of Mr. Tarkington's talent. Subtle and elaborate analysis of the complexities and perversities of the artistic temperament is a field, naturally, much worked by writers of a complex artistic temperament and an introspective method. Mr. Tarkington doubtless deliberately avoids what a number of his characters refer to as the habit of petty analysis. And as an artist himself he is in effect as direct and simple as a bird is an artist in song. While it was convenient to have the gentleman who tells the story of *The Guest of Quesnay* a "painter fellow," and made quite appropriate in the story many extra, pretty touches of blossoms and color, and sensitive appreciation of women as ornaments, this American of the class of those expatriates who "didn't go home in time," is much more of a gentleman merely than a painter. That he is not only an amateur, but a pure type of amateur, is everywhere apparent; and though his friend Ward is a professional, he is a "society painter" and so not at all of the kingdom of serious art. *The Guest of Quesnay* is not only not at all a portrait of a painter as *Evelyn Innes* is a study of the musical temperament, but the art talk in the book any painter who takes himself seriously would call babble.

Most of the writers who make studies of the artistic temperament take their artists with deadly seriousness, as though there were nothing in the world so momentous as the intricate workings of their souls. Mr. Tarkington seems not to take artists, and intellectuals, very seriously; all of his are amateurs: Crailey Gray is an amateur poet; John Harkless, though dramatically successful, is an amateur country editor; Roger Tabor, who worked in paint "after the Spencerian fashion," is a tragically amateurish figure of an artist; and *B*ibbs certainly is an amateur as an essayist, and would have done surprisingly well, as Doc Gurney observed, if he could have made four or five hundred dollars a year by writing by the time he was fifty.

The essay style of the early part of *The Guest of Quesnay* skillfully shifts in the tenser scenes, as the story mounts to its climax, to (almost) the dramatic form of pure dialogue. The daintily vivacious chapter wherein the indomitable Miss Elliott employs the idea of a drawing lesson as a ruse to call upon the painter at *Les Trois Pigeons* that the two of them may fence with Mr. Earl Percy, is like a tiny one-act play. The melodramatic climax of the story is a very illuminating point in an examination of Mr. Tarkington's conception of the world; but not because of its melodrama. It is because of the intensity of the presentation of the nature of Louise Harman's love for the man to whom she "belongs." It was, as the author says, a whole love, for "she was not only wife, but mother to him." In a newspaper interview some time ago Mr. Tarkington was asked how literature had been affected by the suffrage movement and "feminism." He was reported to have replied (looking up in some surprise), "I haven't heard of any change." Mr. Tarkington's ideal of womankind is always the same, and his interpretation of the phenomena of love never varies, throughout his stories. He sees these things very much as eighteenth century Fielding did; and Louise Harman is a sister heroine to Amelia *Booth*.

One cannot say that Mr. Tarkington's treatment of the theme of the relations of the sexes ever rises to heights of sublime dignity, ever to the level of impassioned poetry, as, for instance, in that famous scene of Meredith's Richard and Lucy in the woods by the lake. And on the other hand, he is about as erotic as Scott. Some of the love in his romances could be called little more than Valentine sentiment. Yet a peculiar charm of his fiction is the sweetness, fidelity and goodness of his womankind, the moral fairness of his leading ladies. He believes in the alchemic power of "a good woman" as he would have readers of *The Guest of Quesnay* believe in Professor Keredec. His quaintly adoring, poetic ideal of women as guardians of what is good in men, as some eloquent reviewer has somewhere observed, is an inspiration which gives his earlier books much of their tearful, smiling, tender radiance, their caroling hopefulness.

The women of his ideal are of the sort that give with both hands, rather than receive. The shy, gauche Ariel Tabor, returned from Europe transformed into a vision of feminine grace and charm, gives to Joe Louden the one needful incentive to keep him from weakening at the crucial moment of his fight to conquer Canaan. Mary Vertrees gives to Bibbs the spirit to find music in the hitherto loathed zinc-clipping-machine. And the more "down" their lovers are the more Mr. Tarkington's heroines consider it a point of their womanhood to stand by them. When Ethel Simpson, in *The Man from Home*, perceives the rascality of the situation of her betrothal she feels bound to her affianced by his very dishonor, which she believes it her place to share. While the noble feminine character which Mr. Tarkington, along with the rest of the world, so greatly admires cannot with justice be said to be absent from life, still it need hardly be said that Mr. Tarkington, even in his satirical realism, has never in his fiction been inclined to abandon that very humanly appealing convention of the early novel,—the "heroine," companion figure to his "hero." The saintly heroine, it may be remarked, has ever been an artistic weakness in the fiction of men of gallant heart. And Mary Vertrees, in Mr. Tarkington's most ambitions book, is quite as much of a paragon, an angel, as poor Amelia Osborne.

Mr. Tarkington's constant reader is never permitted to lose track of the fact that the adorable woman, whether she be statuesque or dainty, regal or Cinderella, is of the company of the mothers of the race. All the heroines to whom this author gives his own heart are pronouncedly of the maternal type. Helen Sherwood "was a born mother." And in those ebullient days when he wrote *The Gentleman from Indiana*, before Mr. Tarkington in his realism had embraced the virtue of literary restraint, in Miss Sherwood's solicitude about rubbers and umbrellas for surrounding men folk the author certainly piled it on in the glorious matter of her mothering instincts. Fanchon Bareaud, too, would have followed Crailey Gray to the wars "to hold a parasol over him under the dangerous sun, to cook his meals properly, to watch over him with medicines and blankets and a fan"; her heart breaking with the "crucial yearning to mother him." And Laura Madison, heavenly foil to Mr. Tarkington's Becky Sharp, stepped back a little as her lover came toward her in the great greeting: "Ashes had blown upon her, and oh, the old, old thought of the woman born to be a mother! she was afraid his clothes might get dusty if he came too close."

There is, to be noted, too, another salient characteristic of Mr. Tarkington's heroines: there are no Emma McChesnies among them; they are all ladies, the product of a sheltered rearing. And, as with Mary Vetrees, their going to be stenographers would be unthinkable.

Mr. Tarkington's trifles have, so to put it, a rather wide range of musical scale. Next in order of publication after *The Guest of Quesnay*, and the play *The*

Man from Home, came *Beasley's Christmas Party*, which was followed in turn by a very different sort of trifle indeed, *Beauty and the Jacobin*. The Tiny Tim sort of tale, *Beasley's Christmas Party*, may be viewed in an aspect in which it contributes several considerable strokes to building up a portrait of the author as a man at home. In *Who's Who* Mr. Tarkington gives his "home" as North Pennsylvania Street, Indianapolis. And the spirit of the neighborhood of his residence would seem to be celebrated in the description of the part of the state capital, "Mainwright," in which the Honorable David *Beasley* had his "homely and beautiful," big, old-fashioned brick house, "set well away from the street among some splendid forest trees, with a fair spread of lawn." This was in a quiet part of this "metropolis"; business stopped short of it, and "the fashionable residence section had overleaped it, leaving it undisturbed and unchanging, with that look about it which is the quality of few urban quarters, and eventually of none, as a town grows to be a city —the look of still being a neighborhood." Mr. Tarkington, one gathers, has the reputation of being a famous club-man; again and again in his books the reader comes upon what apparently are strong convictions as to what this club-man thinks a house ought to be. "It was impossible to imagine a child's toy wagon left upon a walk or driveway of the New

House" of the Sheridans in *The Turmoil*. "It revealed nothing of the people who lived in it save that they were rich."

There are houses that cannot be detached from their own people without protesting; every inch of mortar seems to mourn the separation, and such a house—no matter what be done to it—is ever murmurons with regret, whispering the old name sadly to itself unceasingly. But the New House was of a kind to change hands without emotion.

And occasionally the reader of the books of this man about the world gets a caustic criticism of the life which is not lived in houses at all. Miss Fanchon, of New York, Long Shore, and Paris, who perhaps found Penrod a bit "boorjaw," was "one of those grown-up little girls, wonderful product of the winter apartment and summer hotel."

The house of David Beasley's was a *house*. "It gave back a great deal for your glance, just as some people do. . . . Or, driving by, of an evening, you would have liked to hitch your horse and go in; it spoke so surely of hearty, old-fashioned people living there, who would welcome you merrily."

It looked like a house where there were a grandfather and a grandmother; where holidays were warmly kept; where there were boisterous family reunions to which uncles and aunts, who had been born there, would return from no matter what distances; a house where big turkeys would be on the table often; where one called "the hired man" (and named either Abner or Ole) would crack walnuts upon a flatiron clutched between his knees on the back porch; it looked like a house where they played charades; where there would be long streamers of evergreen and dozens of wreaths of holly at Christmas-time; where there were tearful, happy weddings and great throwing of rice after little brides, from the broad front steps.

The sentiment of a joyous domestic life, so hilariously expressed in *Beasley's Christmas Party*, would seem to be an atmosphere quite natural to Mr. Tarkington's own existence. In his correspondence with his youthful nephews (some old letters reveal) he frequently addressed them in such manner as "My Dear Sirs," or "Gentlemen of the Guard," or "Share Awfaw," which he explained was "the way the English pronounce 'Cher Enfants,' and means 'Wicked Boys'"; and he had a habit of subscribing himself "Your docile Uncle," "Your descriptive uncle," and so on. One nosing in his library comes upon a volume of early writings by and about himself collected from magazines, together with some picturesque photographs, which bears the inscription from his father: "Selected and bound for Booth Tarkington, by Papa John."

Beasley's Christmas Party is dedicated to James Whitcomb Riley. It might be suspected that there was more in this than its appropriateness to the vein of kindly sentiment in the story, and its theme of interpreting the life of the affections. Lockerbie Street, as well as (perhaps even more than) the neighborhood of the Tarkington homestead, fits the appreciative description of *Beasley's* neighborhood. And one may find more than a hint of Riley in the character of the whimsical, "lovable," "Sol-Smith-Russell-looking" *Beasley*. Though the author disclaims any consciousness, at least, of such an inspiration.

Beasley and the Hunchbergs, which was the earlier title of the story, or rather of an early version of the later story, appeared in a magazine about four years before the book publication. In the earlier form *Beasley*, and little Hamilton Swift and his Hunchbergs were about all there was to the sketch; the pleasant love note, which made of the sketch a story, was (certainly very adroitly) worked up afterward, perhaps in response to a call for a thorough-going Christmas carol. The roundabout evolution of the story perhaps explains the singular style in which it is cast, a style you might call a curiously informal or negligé style, one which (though here again quite appropriate to its purpose) is so strangely unlike this author elsewhere, and so amazingly unlike the style of, for instance, the *penrod* stories.

In *Beasley's Christmas Party*, though Mr. Tarkington continues brilliantly to eschew those delicately tangled emotions experienced by the supreme few, we find numerous turns of thought reminiscent of Mr. James. Is it not a pleasantly Henry-Jamesian glance, this: "I knew at once that she was Miss Apperthwaite, she 'went so,' as they say, with her mother; nothing could have been more suitable." ? We find again Mr. Tarkington's curious attraction toward speaking from out the atmosphere of a profession he never, in the least, was of,—provincial journalism. We find more melodious darkey singing:

Ah met mah sistuh in a-mawnin'.

In the observations of the old negro *Bob*, we find perhaps an increasing humor in Mr. Tarkington's extraordinary gift for impersonating the Afro-American servant. And, a thing of particular interest to our purpose here, we find an early manifestation of Mr. Tarkington's serious interest as an artist in the psychology of childhood. *Beasley's Christmas Party* is not (as at first blush it may appear) purely an orgy of sentiment; nor is the elfin Hamilton Swift a mere Peter Pan sprite. His vagaries are scientifically sound,—as should be recognized by many mothers of precocious children, queer ones. Though it should not be hard to recall mystified parents of some children who have displayed aberrations not dissimilar to those of Hamilton Swift who have thought their offspring awful liars, or insane. Finally, little Hamilton Swift's peculiar faculties resulted from a nervous ailment, and in Mr. Tarkington's tender little sketch of him one begins to discover in this author what altogether seems to be a sort of *flair* of his for nervous diseases.

* * * * * * * *

Mr. H. L. Mencken, in his essay on Dreiser, observes of Indiana that "its literature, in the main, is a feeble romanticism for flappers and fat women." Mr. Tarkington's next "trifle" to appear between covers, the little one-act play designed for the study, *Beauty and the Jacobin,* brilliant, compact, clean cut, and finished in construction, is again colorful romanticism, but romanticism of a sort which evidently seeks to get quite away from being the kind of gum chewed with relish by the ladies mentioned by Mr. Mencken. The author calls his play "an interlude of the French Revolution"; it was revolutionary, too, in a way in marking an early step of revolt in the author's work. Mr. Tarkington himself speaks of it as a "turning point" in his writing.

One of the reviewers of the book remarked that, "with memories of the fascinating charm of *Beaucaire* the reader seizes this little dramatic romance with eagerness, but lays it aside with a sigh—it is not the same." It certainly is not. In *Beaucaire* the intention one feels to have been to make a story that would seem to be a little eighteenth century play,—rosy footlights reflected on the actors' faces, silver filagree work on a lady's fan. *Beauty and the Jacobin* breaks with the pretty, pretty kind of thing. There is a new quality in the texture of the writing, an apparent purpose to avoid write-y writing. The plot here springs directly from character, and the action of the piece is inevitable. *Beauty and the Jacobin* gives evidence of being the first conscious and determined, as it is the first consistent, effort of the author to leave the surface and work from the inside of his characters out.

The women in the author's previous books may be said to have had about them only bits of reality, and then only incidentally and almost accidentally. (And, of course, there had been only bits, too, of a man in the men.) The marvelously beautiful, imperious, selfish, conscienceless Eloise, who lives for those brief moments in which she is under the limelight of publicity, one of three "emigrants" in the time of the Terror on the point of flight to England when overtaken in a garret in Boulogne by a commissioner of the committee of public safety,—this proud, cold, treacherous fury of a lady is the first definite appearance of any real interest of the author's in a *woman* in a book—in the substance of which women (some women), and not dreams, are composed. She is the Beauty, a type "not made by the sumptuous sculpture alone, but by a very peculiar arrogance—not in the least arrogance of mind." To her the most interesting thing about a rose-bush has been that she, Eloise d'Anville, could smell it. "Moonlight becomes important when it falls upon her face; sunset is worthy when she grows rosy in it." And though, of course, there is only a bit of her given, it is all real enough—a bit of the Narcissa woman, the breed which so curiously Mr. Tarkington has come to be inspired to make his particular prey. Eloise d'Anville is the mother of the flirt, Cora Madison, and of the two very real sisters-in-law in *The Turmoil*—though the sisters-in-law are not Narcissas like Cora.

The whole of the little drama is scintillant with wit, delicate, and at times brilliant and somewhat Shavian, which flashes out poignantly against the sombreness of its background. Mr. Tarkington's new implement, his detective-lantern, is flashed on the character of the Beauty in the duel of wits between her and her captor, the Jacobin; she who has espoused the cause of the Republic, has given to it her fortune, and is sure that her name will protect her and her cousins, two proscribed nobles, a brother and sister, who, taking her under her protest, are fleeing for their lives disguised as peasants, and that the republic is so grateful for what she has done that it will grant them any favor she asks; he, "a man wise enough to make a study of women," for reasons of his own incited to malice against her; a dialogue of wit, keen intelligence, stern purpose on his side, and of belief in herself on hers. In the scintillating, scathing, and adroitly turned satire of the Jacobin some very apt things are said about the "soulless beauty." And in the novel *dénouement* most ingeniously the punishment fits the crime.

VII

THERE was a German lad, one of these psychologists, or perhaps he was a philosopher (I don't, at the moment, recollect his name, but doubtless you will recall it), who, several years ago, "up" and wrote a book in which he classified womankind as of two general types, the maternal type and the courtesan type. Shortly after he delivered himself of this gift to scientific thought he went mad, and a bit later (I believe) committed suicide,—but that was his concern, not ours here. One can fancy Mr. Tarkington (though, with evident astonishment at the suggestion, he indignantly denies this "nut"—as he savagely calls the poor German—as the source of his inspiration), one can fancy him, all aglow with the arresting idea, rising from this (more or less) philosophical volume straightway to do the thing in fiction in *The Flirt;* that startlingly probing, gleamingly brilliant, deliciously malicious study of a heartless coquette, a flame of enchantment, effervescent young sorceress whose diet was excitement, the Narcissa woman, Cora Madison, with her Cinderella foil, home-keeping sister Laura. The rather flippant title of flirt is (to me) annoying because it does scant justice to this young woman, and seems a pale, colorless, inadequate sort of word beside her personified heartlessness. A specialist in nervous diseases might describe Cora (in fact, I believe one such did so describe her in a letter to the author) as a case of incipient Narcissism.

Some of the reviewers (probably wanting their Mr. Tarkington sunny as of old) distastefully spoke of *The Flirt* as unpleasant, and the book (I have heard) never "sold," and even (it is said in the "trade") adversely affected the advance sale of the author's two following books. It would have been perfectly easy to have made *The Flirt* a popular book with perfect certainty: Cora could have repented and reformed and in the end everybody have been made glad, had the author not been quite earnestly bent upon being an artist who set himself to portray the insides of a certain type of person. Of course, Cora is unpleasant, that precisely is the pleasant thing about her. And anyone who has had a keen experience of her kind should find a kind of Penrodian satisfaction of revenge in his recognition of the fact that Mr. Tarkington has got this particular type of woman "down cold." The working of Cora's mind is amazingly real. Her domination of the gentle household by her violent nervous collapses, her fury at the "selfishness" of others, her quick recovery from her hysterical fits which leave no effect upon her, but which wreck everyone about her, her revealing of her innate vulgarity in moments of excitement (as in her damning her lover in the scene of the great tantrums), and her frenzy at the thought (which is the thing that most strikes her) that she has been "made a fool of" in the situation into which she has got herself: all this is done with a scientific relish for character. Cora's belief, too, after having caused her father to suffer a stroke of paralysis, that he is "all right," is another stroke that "rings the bell."

The story paints, also, one of Mr. Tarkington's most excellent *genre* pictures, the little life of the domestic circle of the Madisons in Capital City, "that smoky illuminant of our great central levels"; a gentle family in rather straitened circumstances, so much so that summer vacations are a thing undreamed; a guest at dinner presents crucial problems; and no amount of ingenious refurbishing can make the family wardrobe otherwise than shabby, —all with the exception of Cora. We have again, most happily, Mr. Tarkington's Miss Austenish eye, which, figuratively speaking, sees in the occasion of a bad egg for breakfast the inception of a divorce. When Cora desires guests to dinner, they invariably stay, regardless of the panic wrought in the kitchen. Over rickety furniture and crackling walls (the house of the Madisons was, too, one without a bath) she casts the glamour of her rose-like beauty; and, untroubled by the knowledge that mother and sister are patiently slaving at household tasks, and father racking his brains to know how he is to pay for the new party dress that must be finished for next Thursday, she sets the standard of taste in dress for the community; and through endless, idle hours she is complacently willing to shed the light of her beauty upon anything and everything masculine that comes her way. Such is the setting of a chronicle of family jars precipitated for the most part by that luxuriant forerunner of Penrod, Cora's small brother, Hedrick the Pest, domestic savage, who is the only one with the intellectual courage to see through his sister, and who won't "stand for" her at all; Hedrick, handsome, shabby, dirty, aged about thirteen, vociferous of tongue, impudent of phrase, maddeningly tantalizing by the devilish ingenuity with which he breaks in upon "Cora-lee's" side-piazza tête-à-têtes with ambiguous innuendoes; and whose having been "kissed by an idiot" is the occasion of much Chestertonian mirth in the book. Hedrick (with the most flagrantly jilted of Cora's suitors, Ray Vilas) is the chorus, the critical eye, necessary to reveal the monstrous nature of his sister, but, unlike the villain of the piece, Mr. Corliss, he is mighty far from being merely a device to that end. *The Flirt*, Mr. Tarkington confesses, was the first of his books that

Riley liked, as, he says, Riley's artistic conscience "wouldn't let him." Hedrick, however, captured Riley completely, and he liked every book of the author's that followed.

Here, as throughout his books, Mr. Tarkington's hitting off of manners is seasoned with much criticism of architecture. Indeed, a very fair little critical manual of the evolution of domestic architecture, and garden ornament, in the Middle West might be made of excerpts here and there from Mr. Tarkington's stories. In Capitol City we find ourselves in contact with a past, with a city which has had time to shift its architectural enslavement from mansard and cupola to the gables and jig-saw decorations of Queen Anne, and thence to more varied if not more sensible fashions: "The Goth, the Tudor, and the Tuscan had harried the upper reaches to a turmoil attaining its climax in a howl or two from the Spanish Moor." It is in one of the mansard survivals that Mr. Corliss, returning to his native city after many years abroad, finds the high product of civilization, Cora Madison; but the herd of cast-iron deer that once guarded the lawns of such houses as this, "standing sentinel to all true gentry"; whither were they fled? "In his boyhood, one specimen betokened a family of position and affluence; two, one on each side of the front walk, spoke of a noble opulence; two and a fountain were overwhelming." And every here and there in *The Flirt* one perceives the smoke of the oncoming *Turmoil*, the "long, gray smoke-plume crossing the summer sky" and which dropped "an occasional atom of coal" upon Mr. Corliss's white coat. No good burgher ever complained of the smoke or of the "journalistic uprising" which awakened him— simultaneously with thousands of fellow-sufferers— at about half-after five on Sunday morning:

Over the town, in these early hours, rampaged the small venders of the manifold sheets: local papers and papers from greater cities, hawker succeeding hawker with yell upon yell and brain-piercing shrillings in unbearable cadences. . . . The people bore it, as in winter they bore the smoke that injured their health, ruined their linen, spoiled their complexions, forbade all hope of beauty and comfort in their city, and destroyed the sweetness of their homes and of their wives. It is an incredibly patient citizenry and exalts its persecutors.

The Flirt throughout has a good deal of distinction as an interpretive criticism of the social scene as presented in the Middle Western city which is its setting. Mr. James probably would have liked particularly the reflective picture of the dance to which Cora and Laura go; Cora, radiant-eyed, in high bloom, and exquisite from head to foot in a shimmering white dancing-dress, a glittering crescent fastening the silver fillet that bound her vivid hair; Laura in her made-over black lace dress. "Most of the people at this dance had known one another as friends, or antagonists, or indifferent acquaintances, for years, and in such an assembly there are always two worlds, that of the women and that of the men. Each has its own vision, radically different from that of the other; but the greatest difference is that the men are unaware of the other world, only a few of them—usually queer ones like Ray Vilas—vaguely perceiving that there are two visions, while all the women understand both perfectly. The men splash about on the surface; the women keep their eyes open under water. Or, the life of the assembly is like a bright tapestry: the men take it as a picture and are not troubled to know how it is produced; but the women are the weavers." And the book abounds in witty dialogue, which everywhere most ingeniously furthers the movement of the story.

The story, the plot, is again the trouble, the one element of *The Flirt* open to questioning criticism. One does not feel that the plot was introduced for the sake of a plot, on the other hand one may even be inclined to suspect that it was a nuisance to the author, as it certainly is to the reader whose whole attention is keen on the Mephistophelean diagnosis of Cora's character. But some sort of a mechanism was required to exhibit in all its paces the utterly selfish nature of Cora's sex instinct and the effect of such a character as hers—that it destroys everyone with whom it comes into contact—and so the author cooked up his Basilicata oil fields flimflam. Doubtless something violent, something more or less melodramatic, was required; but Ray Vilas's killing himself might have been made to suffice. The swindling scheme of a fictitious tract of rich oil wells in the heel of Italy, belonging to a non-existent Neapolitan prince, eager to finance a company on a large scale, and unwilling to admit his fellow-countrymen to the secret, seems pretty transparent, too, (and unnecessarily wild and romantic) though it is true that it is frequently surprising what bait people in real life will "bite" on. A duel between Cora and an expert in the same line is effective and no doubt indispensable, but in the suspicious sleekness of word and manner of Corliss, who has acquired, through long years of foreign travel, a certain mannerism, a subtle grace of body and Gallic flattery of speech that dazzle Cora with the charm of the exotic and the unknown, the perspicuous reader early scents the touch of the traditional stage villain in him. And the meandering about the scene, in places intolerably prolonged, of Mr. Pryor, that plain citizen, who was "a tiptop spotter for the government" (and of his grotesque and—as far as I can see— quite superfluous daughter), has the effect of halting the very real adventure of the pursuit of the character of Cora to make way for some rather meretricious adventure business. The reader's entertainment in the case of a whole company of the characters in *The Flirt*, Cora, Laura, Hedrick, father and mother Madison (though perhaps they are a bit over gentle), Wade Trumbell, plodding, prosperous business man, whose chief pleasure is to hear himself talk, is what Mr. James spoke of as the pleasure of recognition; while the Mr. Pryor doings is a horse of the opposite color: there we have the kind of fiction in which the entertainment is designed to result from mystery and surprise. Mr. Pryor is a straw-stuffed figure; and his appearance among the burghers of Capitol City is in effect very much as though you should go to a play by Oscar Wilde and, after a scene or so, on should come a pirate fitted out with a spyglass and cutlass.

So, in *The Flirt*, we see a trace of the glowing romanticist yet remains in the searing satirist into which Mr. Tarkington is emerging, and so also remains a good measure of the generous warmth of kindly heart of the author of *The Gentleman from Indiana*. Offset against this unpleasant and ill-fated pair, the flirt and her rascal, are Laura and Richard, whose story, in so far as it can be detached from that of Cora and Corliss, is, as some reviewer observed, simple and romantic enough to have been conceived by the author of *Little Women*. . . . Mr. Tarkington says that he "might" be able to re-read parts of *The Flirt;* as it was written only five years ago it still seems "possible."

The new Tarkington, Doctor Tarkington the vivisectionist, certainly comes wholly into view in the author's extraordinary boy cycle, which began with Hedrick Madison. There is an unconscionable amount of boy stuff published right along, but only a few of the boys in books have genuine boy insides. The classics are soon numbered; Aldrich's *Story of a Bad Boy*, William Allen White's *Boyville Stories*, Mark Twain's *Adventures of Tom Sawyer*, Mr. Howells' *The Flight of Pony Baker*, and Stephen Crane's few sketches, these are the authentic boy pictures that most readily come to mind. There are, of course, different kinds of boys, as there are different kinds of men and women. Some boys are "little gentlemen," like Georgie Bassett. And some men are old women. But there are certain animal juices in boys which make them distinct among their species; and since the advent of Tom Sawyer and Huckleberry Finn the *boy* in the boy nature certainly has not been so vividly portrayed as in the spectacle of Penrod Schofield and Sam Williams going about their affairs. The Penrod stories are, of course, of the *genre* of Huckleberry Finn, which is mainly to say that Penrod is an intensely American boy. It's a curious thing about boy literature: as the boy, like the man, is an animal distinct from all others, so the American boy, like the North American Indian, it would seem, is of a race like no other. An elaborate autobiographic account of the boyhood of the hero has been a very pronounced feature of recent English fiction; but the youthful Englishman, generally studious and with his thoughts more upon Oxford than upon a show exhibiting a dog part alligator, certainly does not seem to be the cheerful incarnation of natural instinct which was born along the Mississippi River, and later, in somewhat better clothes and a rather more advanced social environment, flourished in Hoosierdom.

Hedrick Madison unconsciously, and without "thinking it out," recognized the naturalness of Cora's seizing upon the deadliest weapon against him that came to her hand. Mr. Tarkington's interpretation of the creature, boy, has a weird quality; and, one has an uncanny feeling, his studies in boy psychology call for some sort of a pathological explanation. In effect his analysis of the utterly mad workings of the boy's mind and the throbbing of his inflamed nerves is as if a boy himself had suddenly become endowed with the faculty of thinking it out aloud. That is, the author's interpretation of the boy, moving about in what is to him the cataclysm of life, does not so much seem to be the work of a mind observing him from without, as it appears to be a voice from within explaining the matter, the voice of a boy uniquely gifted with the power of self-analysis. It is as if the author had a device in his head like the plumbing giving hot and cold water to a bath-tub, and as if he could at will turn off the stream of mature thinking and turn on the boy thinking. And to recapture the sensations of twelve or of seventeen is exactly what the normal adult mind cannot do. Mr. Tarkington's earlier books might have been produced by any brilliant young writer had he happened to possess this particular author's personality, but for the production of his boy stories something else was required, something for which I really know no other name than genius, though that is a deuce of a word to have to use. However, to talk you have to use what words we have. And a genius, according to the most modern theories, bears a relationship to the so-called trance medium: he goes into a sort of trance, and produces work which no other person can produce by the mere application of skill and labor. The author of Penrod and William Baxter certainly is not as other men; he commands some occult power. And the joke of this mystery is that Mr. Tarkington says boy stories are the "easiest" things to write there are. He can "do any of them" in a day and a half. And he thinks that "anybody could do it."

While there is no deficiency of zest in Mr. Tarkington's analysis of the adult character, he seems to go on a kind of a debauch of insight when his mind takes up the subject of juvenile doings; and he becomes possessed of almost demoniac inspirations for hidden truth. He is positively gory in his relish of the exercise of his uncanny power. Like the oft-celebrated fat boy of *Pickwick*, he seems to exult inordinately in making our flesh creep by his amazing and incomprehensible clairvoyance. He appears to become intoxicated by the easy exercise of his singular gift, and piles performance upon performance, each one in stunning effect mounting beyond the last. His small boy is a naïve and spontaneous savage; he is insane; and, at heart, a criminal. He has "a highly developed capacity for pain"; and lives largely in a state of intense agony; he broods profoundly and his brightest thought is revenge; and his humor is indeed "sometimes almost intrusive." His fervent love is a pure passion, honest, innocent, a high exultation, an anguish, and a pain. His life is a keen adventure, a boisterous comedy, and a fearful tragedy. And the wonder of the thing is that your immense entertainment consists of a continuous repetition of shocks of recognition of the veracity of the whole affair. Why is it all so outrageously funny? The most striking thing about the humor of the *Penrod* stories and of *Seventeen* is the effect of the complete absence on the author's part of any effort to be comic. There is nothing at all of the *Peck's Bad Boy* kind of spirit. Penrod and Sam are but automatons of instinct, meaning no evil. They are never "bad." They are something which is not their fault; they are historic. When they throw a stone at the fleeing horse this is a survival of primeval man, who must take every chance to get his dinner, a response to an impulse thousands and thousands of years old—"an impulse founded upon the primordial observation that whatever runs is likely to prove edible." The author is not like a man telling a funny story, but like a man bent with immense earnestness upon telling you the truth; he goes on with a perfectly straight face, solemnly, almost savagely, relating a lot of facts, while you very nearly cry with mirth. In this respect, in the absence in them of the jocose note, it might be argued that *Penrod* and *Seventeen* are superior to *Tom Sawyer* and *Huckleberry Finn*, as in those classics one *is* inclined to feel something of the air of the conscious humorist.

In his boy stories Mr. Tarkington has got hold of a very striking style, a style which though very much a style is one that the reader who has a notion that "style" is something supplementary to, and distinguishable from, matter, would probably regard (with approval) as no style at all. And it is largely because the style of these stories is, so to say, no style at all, no costume in which the thought is dressed, that it is so fine merely as style. It imposes no film of consciousness of itself between the mind of the reader and that of the writer, but is like a wire conductor carrying an electric current between the two. It is composed of a series of terse, absolutely clear, energetic statements, as direct and practical in effect as a market report in a trade journal. It is a medium designed for handling what the newspaper man terms "live news." Its distinction resides in its extraordinary clarity and its eye-opening energy of expression. Every word is the right shot to hit the bulls-eye. Altogether, it is in effect like a series of pistol-like concussions of thought. At least, that is as well as I can analyze it.

Nothing is more extraordinary than the element of personal equation. Though *Seventeen* immediately became one of the most popular books in the world, sundry persons have been reported,—always persons who had never themselves been hobbledehoys,—who could not see anything at all in it. I should myself be tempted to pronounce it about the funniest book in the language. But you cannot altogether explain the fascination exercised by Mr. Tarkington's clairvoyance into primary natures on the ground that many readers have been boys; many readers have not been dogs or colored men. And the ticking of the soul of Duke and of Genesis holds one almost as spell bound as the revealed heart of Penrod and of William Baxter.

Round Mr. Tarkington's luminary, the boy, always revolve his natural satellites the dog and the darkey. The fates which so well looked after, and catered to, the talent of this author saw to it that he was born in not only a Middle Western city, a sort of junction of the manners of the east and of the west, but a city which is practically a Southern city as well; where the barbers, the coachmen, the nurse-maids, and the waiters are "colored." Every native of Indianapolis has been familiar from infancy with the negro man of all work who cuts the grass and sprinkles the lawn. Mr. Tarkington's series plumbing the boy from twelve to seventeen also has the effect of running the whole gamut of the career of the negro servitor, of presenting the seven ages of colored man. His strange life passes in review from the time of the aboriginal Herman and Verman, through the heyday of the colored manhood of Genesis, and takes a look in at the declining light in the "Pappy" of Genesis, with a "cat'rack" in his "lef'" eye, whose "rickaleckshum," of his wives and other things, extends back only to when he was "'bout" fifty. But, feat upon feat, Mr. Tarkington, in his lust for mimicry not content with the fantastic language of Herman, makes Verman tongue-tied!

As a member of what might be called the dog

school of writers Mr. Tarkington is decidedly "different." We have a large and continually increasing body of dog literature, of which *Bob, Son of Battle, The Bar Sinister*, and *The Call of the Wild* are the classic examples. And this literature is almost wholly the extreme of sentimental romanticism. The dog in fiction is nearly always a glamorous hero. Usually he is a very famous character—everybody in Alaska (or wherever the scene of his exploits is) has heard of him. How he became the leader of the pack, or saved somebody's life, or flagged a train on the brink of the broken bridge, or put out a fire with his teeth, or made good in some spectacular way is the climax of a tale replete with thrills, and in which sobs over his sublime love of man are not spared. Mr. Tarkington stands somewhat solitary as a realist in the dog line,—as, you might say, the dog's George Gissing. There are no purple patches on his dogs. One very human thing about his dogs is that they are lowly, and humble. Duke's name "was undescriptive of his person, which was obviously the result of a singular series of mesalliances. He wore a grizzled moustache and indefinite whiskers; he was small and shabby, and looked like an old postman." Clematis was a dog "that would have been recognized anywhere in the world as a colored person's dog. He was not a special breed of dog—though there was something rather houndlike about him—

he was just a dog. His expression was grateful but anxious, and he was unusually bald upon the bosom, but otherwise whitish and brownish, with a gaunt, haunting face and no power to look anybody in the eye." Of course, there is Flopit, too; but Flopit, though aristocratic, is a simpleton.

Dogs are sprinkled along in Mr. Tarkington's books in about the same proportion that, I guess, they are found in life. One can readily lay hand on a dog almost anywhere. Perhaps as good an example as another of the curious mental telepathy apparently existing between Mr. Tarkington and dogs is expressed in the Rupe Collins chapter of *Penrod:*

Duke could chase a much bigger dog out of the Schofields' yard and far down the street. This might be thought to indicate unusual valour on the part of Duke and cowardice on that of the bigger dogs whom he undoubtedly put to rout. On the contrary, all such flights were founded in mere superstition, for dogs are even more superstitious than boys and colored people; and the most firmly established of all dog superstitions is that any dog—be he the smallest, feeblest in the world—can whip any trespasser whatsoever. . . . A rat-terrier believes that on his home grounds he can whip an elephant.

For the well proportioned world that they mirror, comparatively few cats are to be seen in Mr. Tarkington's pages. Way back in *The Gentleman from*

Indiana histrionically comical Wilkerson swung, as a sort of artistic pendulum, "an unhappy mongrel" dog at the tail of the column marching against the Cross Roads. This ancient animal was of Mr. Tarkington's favorite dog color, yellow. The "fuzzy, white ball" which Miss Betty Carewe carried one morning in "a world all sunshine and green leaves" was, first, a pawn necessary to Fate, and, secondly, it was merely a water-color kitten in a sentimental water-color picture. Any former neglect of cats by this author, however, is completely atoned for in his history of that theatre of war which was the back yard of Penrod shared by Sam. There is a Cat worthy of—whom shall we say?—Zola?—no, Mr. Tarkington; such a villainous cat as has not elsewhere terrorized the readers of a book: Gipsy (its name in the days when it had a home), that cat "needlessly tall, powerful, independent, and masculine;" who wanted free air and free life, the lights, the lights, and the music; and who abandoned the bourgeoisie irrevocably, by going forth in a May twilight, carrying the evening beefsteak with him, and joining the underworld.

VIII

IT was, I suppose (looking back), in this way that I got started on the idea of writing this essay, in which I, at least, have found for the mind considerable of what one Quinney called "meat and gravy."

I have made an extensive study of clubs. I collect clubs, as you may say; not in the sense that I belong to many, but in this: that I make it a point to possess with my mind the cosmopolitan variety I have seen. One of the most winning clubs, then, in my collection is one that I picked up, so to say, in Indianapolis, the University Club there. For one gracious thing it is housed in one of those mellow, old architectural piles, a type of old time mansion specimens of which are frequently found in Indiana, which connote to the reflective mind the period of the civil war, a house which in the sentiment of its effect is like to a gentleman of the old school; and it stands on the patrician and park-like North Meridian Street in a dainty little lawn. To the original two-story, red-brick building has been added a third story perfect in its recognition of the distinction of character of the original design. Within the high-ceilinged rooms of this simple, noble, one-time residence broods an atmosphere from out the past of old-fashioned culture. A much pleasanter place altogether, certainly more soothing, than the stately and mighty Reform Club.

I was sitting in the University Club at Indianapolis, reading the paper, when a voice of hoarse timbre and of unusual volume sounded out in the hall, and a young man with a good deal of something about him entered the room. I know not exactly what name to put upon this something, perhaps you would call it "class." A young man in that he may have been anywhere between thirty-five and forty-five (or so). College chap kind of look. He was fashionably dressed and carried a handsome cane. Several persons who had been drowsing burst into hearty welcome; and there came instantly into the atmosphere an electric feeling of something unusual going forward. In a hearty fashion the newcomer cordially returned all greetings. He had, apparently, just got back after an absence from the city.

Seated presently, he had very much the effect, with his slouched attitude and his smart apparel, of a portrait, So-and-So, Esq., that you might see at, say, the Montross Gallery. He was drawn into conversation by an elderly character nearby, whose appearance suggested an old-fashioned judge of a Circuit Court. This engagingly musty-looking person evidently considered literature a suitable topic of conversation with the young man, and he fell to a discussion of John Ruskin, of whom, it seemed, he was very fond. Now I felt that faint feeling at my stomach which I always feel whenever I expect that I am about to be awfully bored. I have never been able to read any of John Ruskin, and it has been my opinion that nobody does read him, except, possibly, elderly gentlemen who look like old-fashioned judges of Circuit Courts.

The hoarse, hearty, richly dressed young man, however, quite astonished me. He was not bored in the least. You might have thought (though I afterward learned that he "hates" John Ruskin) that John Ruskin had been meat and drink, wife and child, music and smoking tobacco to him throughout his life. The picturesque old codger with much deference frequently addressed the dashing young blade as "Mr. Tarkington." And this Mr. Tarkington was very keen, it appeared, on a matter which he continually named—art. He discoursed of rhythm, which, he insisted, was as much a property of prose as of verse. And he held that, commonly, critical judgment had little to do with the case: one liked or disliked an author according to the degree one vibrated, or did not vibrate, in sympathy with the rhythm of that author's writing. The rhythm of some authors was "congenial" to one, others not. "Well," I said to myself, "all this rather gets my goat!"

You see, at that time I had somehow never pictured to myself Booth Tarkington as at heart torn by the anguishing problems of Flaubert. I had got it into my head that he was a "popular novelist," a society butterscotch, one who carried lightly a jolly bright talent. A deep sea monster, not exactly! The thing about him, now that I had him before me, that particularly appalled me was his deadly earnestness. I don't know that I have ever seen a man who appeared to be more hell-bent, which is the only way that puts it exactly, on what he believed to be so.

Next (I don't remember just how he got to that subject) he "went for" Indianapolis. "Dirt, smoke and rotten politics," that was all it was. "I have a book now running in *Harper's*," he began. . . . "Then why do you come back here?" inquired the old gentleman, with, it must be confessed, some point. "To work!" was the searing reply. "I can work only in a dirty, dark, dull place." His house had been robbed three times within the last several weeks; you might think he was running "some kind of a home for burglars"; he had been held up at a pistol's point on his own block; a forest of telegraph poles had been planted before his door while he was away,—and the city's office holders were "playing checkers at the fire engine house." The hoarse young man appeared to be somewhat "sore." The admirer of Ruskin was advised, with a good deal of intensity, to read the book in *Harper's*, though, unfortunately, it would probably not be much read here, and it was sadly emasculated by the requirements of present-day publication. He was also informed in this connection that nothing was known about literature at universities, where old bones were dissected with profound solemnity. . . . My desire to talk with so spirited a creature was growing prodigiously.

In a succinct note, in reply to my request to "meet" him, I was invited to call at the Tarkington homestead on North Pennsylvania Street. It's a fine way, I think, for a man to have his home, at the seat of his family, in the house of his father, and his father's fathers. I had some time to wait before the master of the house arrived; and I surveyed a curious sort of apartment whose conglomerate paraphernalia suggested that it might have been got together by Stanford White. It seems to me that there were things such as these there: huge, stone Italian mantels; massive, carven, gargoyle-like chairs; early primitive Italian painting; and a great deal of, I should say, that sort of thing.

After a bit a fancy dog appeared (not a yellow dog, not at all a colored person's dog, but a large and aristocratic-looking, black poodle, shaven in some places and tufted in patches) and in its wake came Mr. Tarkington, in a sweater, I think, and got up as though for knocking about in the country. Directly following a hearty handshake, I was presented with the first of a succession of enormous cigarettes bearing in giant letters (for a cigarette) the initials "B. T." These paper-encased torpedoes their owner carried upright in his breast pocket, as you do cigars. Now, you might expect a strikingly humorous and abundantly witty writer to be rather a witty man in his talk; but, as far as I could make out, this particular humorist, satirist, what you will, is so bloomin' sincere that he forgets all about scintillating when he talks. Standing on his hearth-rug before me, with his legs wide apart, his comedian's mask drooping forward like a bloom on its stalk, and standing so suggesting to my mind the idea of the master of some baronial hall, he gave me a lengthy and a rather dry lecture on the function of book reviews and the duties of reviewers,—reviewing being my calling. Mr. Tarkington is one of those authors who never read reviews of their own work; at least, he "tries" not to; but when they are sent to him by friends, and he has them in his hand, he "of course can't help it."

His acquaintance with reviews has apparently left him with the impression that his reviewers have seldom read the book. For a reviewer "to have read the book and have emerged with an intelligent impression of what the author was about, that is the important thing to the novelist and to the reader who wants the reviewer to give him some notion of the book,"—"I should not put the novelist first!" says Mr. Tarkington. Such a review, one which "proves the understanding and thoroughness of the reviewer," is as "good" a review as one may hopefully ask for. Evidently he has been much exasperated by reviewers "blandly stating things with complete incorrectness, thus demonstrating the most hurried skimming." Such a reviewer has "floundered, shirked his job, and then tried to cover bad work with dishonesty." "A reviewer should understand that he reviews himself also, shouldn't he?" Once, it appears, a reviewer misquoted a word in a line of one of Mr. Tarkington's books. And Mr. Tarkington "suggested" that "a painful and restless sensitiveness to words is as necessary to the reviewer as to the novelist."

It so falls out that I have lived a good part of my life among painters, professors, newspaper men, journalists, poets, publishers' literary advisers, book sellers, and writers of books. With the exception of the painters, of such a man, for instance, as John H. Twachtman, I think I have never heard any one so frequently refer to "the artist" as did Mr. Tarkington as to an ideal. How do wars affect literature? as the interviewer now continually asks. With Mr. Tarkington the matter altogether comes back to the nature of the artist. Regardless of wars the artist will go on giving expression to himself and his reaction to the things about him, as he has ever done. And so on.

And he told me a number of stories, like a commercial traveller in a smoking car or an after-dinner speaker. "Mr. Tark-ing-ton" (as with a sonorous sound he names himself), said the doctor, and so and so. And then he said to the doctor such and such. Like that! I wish I could remember the one about George Ade and an English actor in China or South Africa or some such place. As to that dirt, smoke and rotten politics business, it is those who really care for this land whose wrath is toward her now. Twenty, thirty, or more years ago this city was a pleasant place in which to live. Our fathers suffered, and toiled, and builded and bled, that we should come into our inheritance—for this, a turmoil! The outstanding features of this striking man, I felt to be a remarkable energy of feeling, and a quick and generous sympathy with anything like "hard lines" in the situation of another.

I had recently "busted down," largely as the result of a too continuous application of mind. Mr. Tarkington's ready and patently genuine concern as to this affair of mine somewhat startled me. No, certainly, I could not stand such a routine grind. (I knew this man understood the "artist.") And he told me how after a round at writing he was "limp." I recalled Mr. Nicholson's description of his (Mr. Tarkington's) manner of working. Lock himself up in a room two or three days running; believed he slept a few hours in the night on a couch there; had a little food brought in to him now and then; refused to budge from the spot until he was spent. There pops into one's head Mr. Brownell's saying, in a beautiful figure, of Hawthorne writing *The Scarlet Letter* that "he shut himself up and wrestled continuously with the angel of his inspiration till he had conquered."

Then I began to find that when Mr. Tarkington writes you a letter, or at least when he writes me a letter, he writes just like the correspondent of a business house,—though, we know, he never had a job anywhere in his life. Except that his handwriting is awful. And apparently he does all his letter writing by hand. His capital "I"s are all capital "Y"s. And he signs himself simply "N. *B.* Tarkington," which is an admirable thing to do, I think, because it has a practical, no-monkey-business sound, and nothing of the "J. Shameous O' Field" literary name kind of thing about it. His epistolary statements I have found all very earnest, as though he had his nose (that noble nose of the humorist) very close to the paper.

Monsieur Beaucaire, according to Mr. Frederic Taber Cooper writing in 1911, "immediately, once and for all, defined Mr. Tarkington's proper sphere and limitations." The hoodwinked critic was, very painstakingly, surveying the talent of the author of eight books then published, which concluded with *The Guest of Quesnay;* and thus, of course, was at a very great disadvantage. It is entertaining to note that it then seemed that that "dainty bit of fictional artistry," *Beaucaire,* "proved" Mr. Tarkington "one of those writers whose stories, whenever and wherever laid, should carry with them something of the 'once-upon-a-time' atmosphere,—the fictional atmosphere of the story that aims frankly to entertain." Further, "it reduced at once to an absurdity the bare idea of Mr. Tarkington's ever again attempting to write a novel opening with such prosaic actuality as 'There is a fertile stretch of flat lands in Indiana where unagrarian Eastern travelers, glancing from car-windows, shudder and return their eyes to interior upholstery.'"

It is perhaps something more than a simple coincidence that Mr. Tarkington's most mature effort, a far cry indeed from a dainty bit of fictional artistry and a once-upon-a time atmosphere, should hark straight back to his maiden volume, and begin:

"There is a midland city in the heart of fair, open country, a dirty and wonderful city nestling dingily in the fog of its own smoke." Apparently the idea was to do the same picture over again in different colors, and this time, with increased knowledge and power, to do it right. The keynote, however, struck in each of these two opening, or "topic," sentences is distinctly opposite one from the other. If there was any element of combat in the earlier volume (and an article in praise of the Middle West which the author contributed to a magazine at about that time suggests that there may have been) the resentment, in defense of his own, was directed against a sense of superiorness felt in the East. In the second case not a champion is needed, but a critic of the "dirty city nestling dingily in the heart of its own smoke." It will also be perceived that his second opening sentence is a much better sentence than the first, a quicker, more compact and nervous "prose." And it immediately proceeds to a tone not before felt, with anything like this intensity, anywhere in the author's work. There is a grim ring, resonant of pomp and panoply, to the firmly marching passages that follow. The air is lowering, ominous, and as the pages turn, the reader feels something of an epic roll to the lines, a Thackerayan rumble in the distance, a reminiscence of Vanity Fair with Waterloo looming beyond. The ground trembles with the force of moral indignation. The effect is incontestably impressive, and the genuineness and fervor of the inspiration voiced in chapter one are indubitable. Has this inspiration the vitality to drive straight to the end?

In considering *The Turmoil* it is interesting, if nothing more, to remember Mr. Tarkington's preacher grandfather, "one of the fathers of Indiana Methodism," as a quaint old volume, *Indiana Methodism*, by a brother pioneer preacher (and a grandfather, by the way, of the present writer), calls him. The Reverend Joseph Tarkington contributed to this volume his own sketch of his life and times. And there are moments in the sonorous roll of the righteous sentences of this distinguished gentleman of another day when he reveals something of the bright humor of his celebrated grandson. In his account, for instance, of a "camp meeting" to which he went as a child "to cry for mercy," he confesses that, "It had been my desire that the Lord would bless me in private, and in a peculiar manner, and my prayers had been directed to this end; but before the blessing came, I was willing to receive it in any manner, and on any terms."—A line, one recognizes, which might easily have been written by the novelist.

For the most part, however, this narrative is a story of the rugged school in which moral fibre was welded. Young Joseph Tarkington went on his wedding tour, not to Niagara and to the White Mountains, nor to Lake Superior or to California, but to *Conference*. And if lithe humor and a command of the written word flowed in the line of the Tarkington blood, so (as one sees in the "morals" of Mr. Tarkington's stories) did a didactical strain of a lofty ethical ideal and a strong sense of moral values. And whatever may have been the source of the note of a sound, old oaken philosophy which may have been perceived growing more and more perceptible in Mr. Tarkington's work, the "Hoosier Olympian" (in Mr. Nicholson's happy phrase descriptive of the rugged pioneers who planted the garden in the Hoosier wilderness) who was his grandsire—one of the old line Indianaians nurtured on the pap of the *Bible*, the spirit of the Civil War, and rousing Indiana "preaching"—might have delivered in another form from his pulpit (had he suddenly returned) the thesis of *The Turmoil*. Further, Mr. Tarkington's intimacy with the Scriptures will have been remarked in many an apt allusion here and there throughout his work, and an echo of the *Biblical* rhythm noted in an occasional turn of phrase. And as *The Turmoil* unrolls it is impossible to fail to perceive that the beat of the style is Old Testament.

The Turmoil, which, later, Mr. Tarkington felt called upon to "explain" in his magazine article

"Vreedersburgh—The City Beautiful," bears an amusing analogy to *Gulliver's Travels*, in that it has been very widely enjoyed under something very like, presumably, a misapprehension. The savage Dean's gospel of hatred, his testament of woe—upon which he expended the treasures of his wit, and into which he instilled the concentrated essence of his rage at the animal man—has become a child's book, and has been read with wonder and delight as a fascinating fairy tale by generations of innocents. No one could take Mr. Winston Churchill's *A Far Country*—which, curiously enough, appeared almost simultaneously with *The Turmoil*—for anything other than what it is: an indictment of modern American conditions in the commercial life of big cities. Mr. Tarkington's novel of flamingly didactic inspiration, his unsparing diagnosis of the great American disease of the love of Bigness, has been labeled by one impressionable reviewer thus: "No more beautiful story of young love has ever been conceived." Naïve testimony, at any rate, to the author's potency as a novelist, whatever he may have "on his chest" in the way of a "message."

Booksellers and librarians have confessed to having been puzzled to account for some sort of hypnotic quality apparently possessed by *The Turmoil*. It has had, such persons state, an effect little short of unheard of before. It has been given to all whose request was for "a good story," and instead of the usual number of such persons coming back with the familiar remark that that book was "no good," and the threatening command not to give them any such book again, while yet others were highly pleased; in this case the verdict was unanimous, and the respouse was a general call for another book "like that." These highly satisfied customers comprised many varieties of type, with perhaps "flappers and fat women" predominating. Though it is said that business men, too, probably "young business men," like the lampooned Roscoe and Jim Sheridan, found the book very agreeable. Why they thought it was so "good," doubtless very few of all those who enjoyed it could have said. And Professor Phelps' critical dictum that it "has proven that the author can write a novel full of cerebration without losing any of his charm," does not, it may be felt, get much forrader. Probably the simplest explanation of the effect so universally felt of its being such a good book is that *The Turmoil* has first, last, and all the time, the nervous vitality of life. It has this to a degree far and away beyond any other of Mr. Tarkington's books. A sense of the vibration of the press of life from all four sides is conveyed in a measure beyond that to be felt in any other American novel that can readily be named. In its signal presentation of the brunt of American life to-day, *The Turmoil*, one is tempted to say, is the most successful approximation in sight to the thing prophesied in that venerable mirage, the Great American Novel.

The Turmoil is a thoroughly modern form of a very old kind of story, the Parable of the old Jewish literature. It tells of a City, where wealth is loved better than cleanliness, where the citizens have lost their old neighborliness and simplicity in their rush for money, where Bigness is the only god known; a place where honor, poetry, truth and beauty are almost forgotten, where law is a joke, the rulers venial, and the citizens heartless. It is a writing on the wall of the City, a voice speaking against the crassly materialistic spirit which animates this epitome of our urban civilization, against the spirit which finds garish and noisy expression in municipal "slogans," municipal "boosting" and municipal advertisement, against that sort of cheap and nunatural civic enthusiasm which is vulgar (in the modern sense of the word). And in the personality of Sheridan, something big, powerful, and ugly, that must have something behind it, some meaning, the Parable dramatizes "the city incarnate." "It was Narcissism in him to love the city so well; he saw his reflection in it; and, like it, he was grimy, big, careless, rich, strong, and unquenchably optimistic."

In its outline the story goes back to a time before the parable. Here we have the simple fairy story of the King and his three sons—the great financier Sheridan and Bibbs and his two elder brothers. In accordance with the ancient tradition, the youngest son is an "ugly duckling" and turns out to be a swan. One of the brothers dies: "Standing in the black group under gaunt trees at the cemetery, three days later, Bibbs unwillingly let an old, old thought become definite in his mind: the sickly brother had buried the strong brother, and Bibbs wondered how many million times that had happened since men first made a word to name the sons of one mother." The other brother becomes a drunkard, and Bibbs, made whole and strong, wins the high-born lady's love—but does he live happy ever after? A reviewer in the New York *Times* has poetically found in Bibbs more than Sheridan's son: he is, it may be, the Soul of Man. And the story, thus, is of the conflict between the City and the Soul, the City striving to crush the Soul or else to mould it into its own hideous image. And "the Soul triumphs by the aid of—well, what is Mary Vertrees? Beauty, or Truth, or Love?" But the soul of Bibbs (though he, being after all the son of his father, had a good deal of the obstinacy of the elder mule) certainly does not triumph; and the story, many of its readers doubtless would be surprised to hear, does *not* have a "happy ending." There is no evidence that Bibbs ever became a great business man—he did well enough to please his father, who was astonished that (in Dr. Johnson's figure about the dancing dog) he could walk on his hind legs at all. There is, further, a very strong suggestion that the thesis of the story is completed by the implication that much brains are not required to be a business man, particularly if you have behind you as much money as the sons of Sheridan had behind them. We leave Bibbs with the prospect of becoming a fair business man, and nothing more, before him.

The author of *The Gentleman from Indiana* expressed a feeling, perhaps a boyish feeling, that Indiana people were sane, kind and without mean and little traits; and, as to that, many native Indianaians of his generation would now say (I have occasion to believe) that he was rather right about it,—about the "old stock," at least. Then, in this "homelike" place, "no one was very rich; few were very poor; the air was clean, and there was time to live." But:

In the souls of the burghers there had always been the profound longing for size. Year by year the longing increased until it became an accumulated force: We must Grow! We must be Big! We must be Bigger! Bigness means Money! And the thing began to happen; their longing became a mighty Will. We must be Bigger! Bigger! Bigger! Get people here! Coax them here! Bribe them!

Swindle them into coming, if you must, but get them! Shout them into coming! Deafen them into coming! Any kind of people; all kinds of people! We must be *B*igger! *B*low! *B*oost! *B*rag! Kill the fault-finder! Scream and bellow to the Most High! *B*igness is patriotism and honor! *B*igness is love and life and happiness! *B*igness is Money! We want *B*igness!

They got it. From all the states the people came; thinly at first, and slowly, but faster and faster in thicker and thicker swarms as the quick years went by. White people came, and black people and brown people and yellow people; the negroes came from the South by the thousands and thousands, multiplying by other thousands faster than they could die. From the four quarters of the earth the people came, the broken and the unbroken, the tame and the wild—Germans, Irish, Italians, Hungarians, Scotch, Welsh, English, French, Swiss, Swedes, Norwegians, Greeks, Poles, Russians, Jews, Dalmatians, Armenians, Roumanians, *B*ulgarians, Servians, Persians, Syrians, Japanese, Chinese, Turks, and every hybrid that these could propagate. And if there were no Eskimos nor Patagonians, what other human strain that earth might furnish failed to swim and bubble in this crucible?

The town had become a city. It scorned art, and it begot a very tolerable work of art,—*The Turmoil.* There used to be, about the time of Verlaine, a tribe of "un-moral" writers who called themselves, or were called, Symbolists, or Decadents, or something like that, and who found the evil and the ugly to be beautiful. They always went to great cities to look for their material. They had their cult, but they were not very popular. The metamorphosis of his town into a city had the same sort of an effect on Mr. Tarkington as an artist as his experience of the sordidness of politics. In considering Mr. Tarkington's "insides" (as he terms the psychology of his characters) it will never do to get away from the fact that the things for which he most earnestly cares are the simple, honest, wholesome, upright things, and those which come of gentle breeding. Except his City of Turmoil, and fair bits of Paris in *The Beautiful Lady* and *The Guest of Quesnay*, he has never put a city into a novel. Though he has been much in New York, and, "purely on business," frequently goes there now, he declares that he knows "very little about even one bit of it"; and apparently he has never felt the special kind of romance of this "Bagdad of the subway." A friend of his, an Easterner (one of those who couldn't live anywhere West of the Hudson River), remarked of him, in an amused way, "He wouldn't live anywhere but in Indianapolis." He seems even to have a prejudice against New York, as in a letter to a friend he speaks of So-and-So's being "from" Kentucky, another man's being from Ohio, another from San Francisco, a fourth he "suspects of having been born in or near New York," but in this case that "is all right."

His special heaven on earth, apparently, is "the water" by his summer home in Maine. And his highly civilized soul, it would seem, answers deep unto deep with the "country." Calling on a friend who lived on the outskirts of Indianapolis, and, in a fancy overcoat, getting out of his limousine, he made as if to leap and shout. Asked why he made as if to leap and shout, he replied, "Why, this is regular country out here!" When it was mentioned that the weather had been bad in the country recently, he declared, "Any kind of weather is fine in the country." There is an art, such as O. Henry's, which finds something very humanly appealing in "grafters," pickpockets, and women of the town. Mr. Tarkington, I should say, is about as likely to write a story about a pickpocket as he is to be one. He would have all things clean, and simple, and "good." Thus, naturally, he was "riled" when in the former sweetness of that place:

The old, leisurely, quizzical look of the faces was lost in something harder and warier; and a cockney type began to emerge discernibly—a cynical young mongrel, barbaric of feature, muscular and cunning; dressed in good fabrics, fashioned apparently in imitation of the sketches drawn by newspaper comedians. The female of his kind came with him—a

MR. TARKINGTON'S STUDY AT KENNEBUNKPORT, MAINE

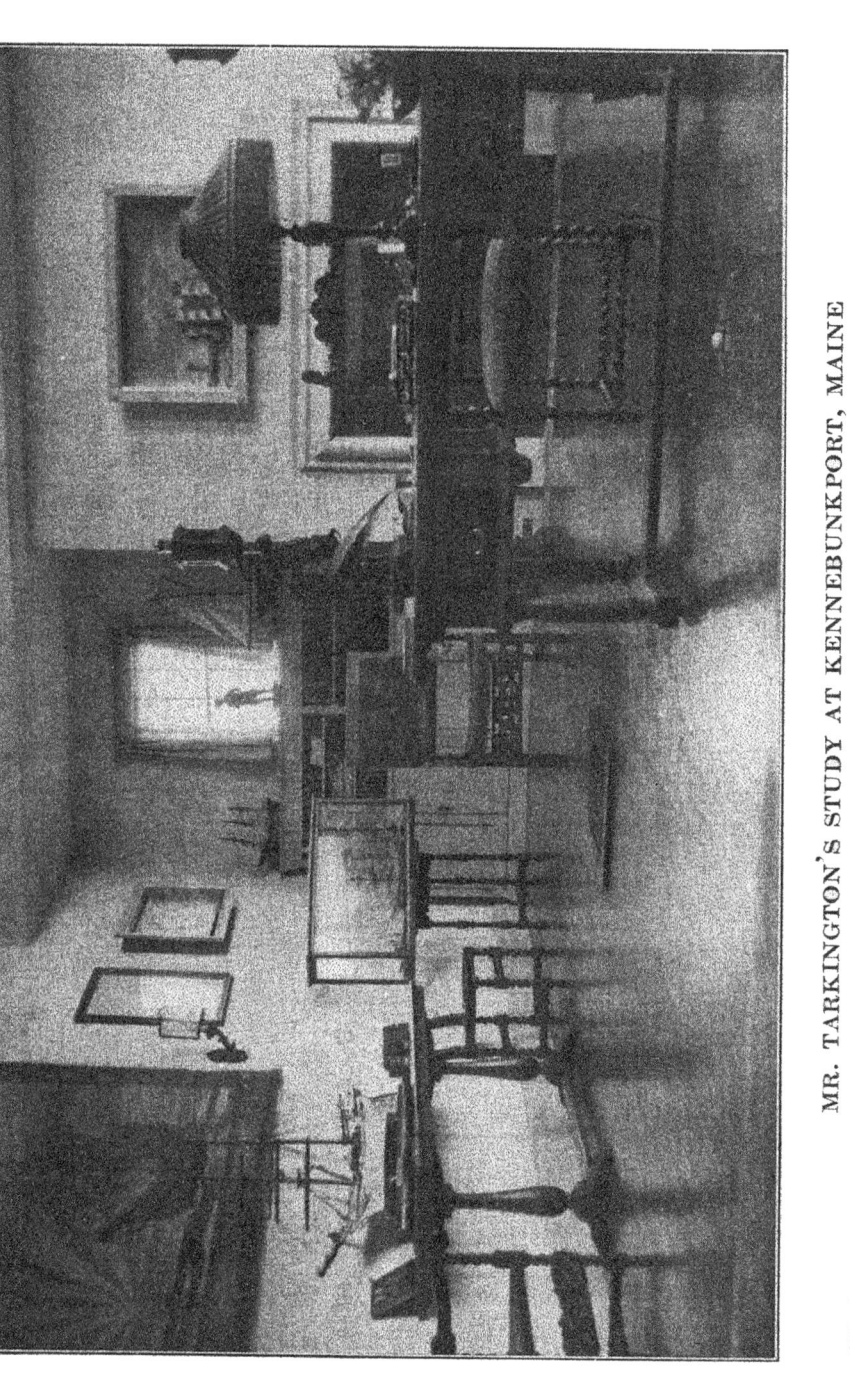

His house overlooks the harbor from which many ships in the old days began their first voyages. Models of vessels of every rig are included in this collection. There is no taint of the "big smoke" in this room.

pale girl, shoddy and a little rouged; and they communicated in a nasal argot, mainly insolences and elisions. Nay, the common speech of the people showed change; in place of the old, midland vernacular, irregular but clean, and not unwholesomely drawling, a jerky dialect of coined metaphors began to be heard, held together by *gunnas* and *gottas* and much fostered by the public journals.

The city piled itself high in the center, tower on tower for a nucleus, and spread itself out over the plain, mile after mile; and in its vitals, like benevolent bacilli contending with malevolent in the body of a man, missions and refugees offered what resistance they might to the saloons and all the hells that cities house and shelter.

Singer, actor, poet, artist, preacher, psychologist, —and now sociologist, for such Mr. Tarkington definitely became in *The Turmoil.* "Of course I should claim that I *am* a sociologist," he has said (somebody had suggested that he had not designed to be), "and I conceive it no particularly dashing claim either. If I were not one my novel could not be true. If a novelist is not a sociologist he is not a novelist, is he?" To the criticism that has been made in one or two places that in his rebellion against the god *B*igness, against the lust for power, wealth, and magnitude which inflames this community which may be taken as one typical of present-day America, and, he holds, has produced in its citizens a sort of spiritual, physical, and mental degeneration; that in this he has made the people of *The Turmoil* more selfish, arrogant, and mercenary than his models really are; that, in short, in his municipal and individual psychology he has overstated his case; to this he retorts: "As a matter of fact, there isn't any answer to the criticism that *The Turmoil* overstates its case. There wouldn't be any answer if a doctor—merely diagnostician in this instance—said 'Typhoid,' and a critic insisted, 'But you didn't notice what a pretty nose the patient has.'" Nor was he gratified at a kindly critic's urging in extenuation of the relentless and devastating nature of his criticism that he promised that the patient would get well, that the city of which he writes, that America, in fact, is merely passing through a phase of growth; that the spiritual conditions described in *The Turmoil* cannot endure. "Either my diagnosis stands," he said shortly after the book was published, "or I have to eat it." Still, behind this something big, ugly, powerful, and "unquenchably optimistic," Sheridan and his city, there must be something, some meaning. At any rate, an incorrigibly Bibbsian vision came to the beaten idealist, *B*ibbs, when, unaware that Love waited him just outside the door, he sat in his office and mused on his enemy, the conqueror, the city of his habitation:

Looking once more from the window, Bibbs sculptured for himself—in the vague contortions of the smoke and fog above the roofs—a gigantic figure with feet pedestaled upon the great buildings and shoulders disappearing in the clouds, a colossus of steel and wholly blackened with soot. But Bibbs carried his fancy further—for there was still a little poet lingering at the back of his head—and he thought that up over the clouds, unseen from below, the giant labored with his hands in the clean sunshine, and Bibbs had a glimpse of what he made there—perhaps for a fellowship of the children of the children that were children now—a noble and joyous city, unbelievably white.

The Turmoil is all of a piece; it drives unswervingly to its appointed end. There is not a touch of claptrap, of melodrama, of purple, in it. It has no essential "situation," no point of "plot" at all,—as a reviewer for a paper which is one of our first literary authorities said it had. Mr. Howells has declared (I have heard) that "no English writer on tiptoe could touch the climax of *The Turmoil*." But at what precise point of the book is there such an artifice as a "climax"? There is no "shaping" at all in the effect of the story. It has grown, in effect, as naturally as a tree; and it has the swing, and rugged balance, and careless symmetry which (contrary to some artistic theories) Nature has. The career of Sheridan is portrayed with the same sort of "composition" that exists in life (was there not "composition" in the life of Napoleon?) and no more. Behind *The Turmoil* everywhere is a remarkable, an amazing, pounding energy of mind. The vehemence of the satire curls the reader's hair. The evolution of the theme, so natural in effect, is positively devilish in its completeness. The idea there elaborated is exhibited kicking with all its four legs in a manner that, one cannot resist saying, could not possibly be better. And the characters are no box of tricks, but people, everyone, hot off the bat, with uncommonly human "insides." And over all is a moving feeling of appreciation of what is fine and of compassion for what is absurd and pitiable.

The elder Sheridan, of course, is the Silas Lampham of his time, the typical self-made American of the era; and if he is not a "speaking likeness," I really don't know where you will go to hear one talking. Conrad's Swede, Axel Heyst, in *Victory*, has been called, most appropriately, "a South Sea Hamlet." Bibbs, I should call, an Indianapolis Hamlet. He has a Hamletic soul, this attractive young man, humorist, dreamer, sicklied o'er with thought. Mary Vertress's only fault is that she is so faultless; but she is not a pale nature. She has a will, this Diana Vernon with a bubbling sense of humor. As a creation Mother Sheridan can only be described as a "peach." The elderly, pinched Mr. Vertrees, left at the post by the modern rush of things, "managing somehow" to maintain his "position in life," whose character is so beautifully reflected in the mirror of his "Landseers," is exquisitely rendered. The two elder brothers, Jim and Roscoe, "capable, hardworking young business men," wearing "young business men's moustaches" and "rich suitings in dark mixtures," are all over the land. Of the humorous, "racially sympathetic" George and Mist' Jackson nothing further is required to be said than that they are "colored." The figure of that "lami*dal*" Moor, it should be noted, plays not only a humorous part, but a scientific part, when crashed by Sheridan to give him relief at the culmination of his otherwise unbearable frenzy,—the same part as that played by Anatole France's wicker-work woman.

The Turmoil is remarkable as a book of nervous diseases, all understood as if with the trained mind of the admirable Doc Gurney. Sheridan, of course, is a victim of the great American disease of money-mania. Bibbs is an invalid, whose malady,—like Stevenson's, is of that peculiar order which seems to contribute to playful spirits and cheerfulness; and his cure is quite scientifically wrought. Roscoe is Mr. Tarkington's most thoroughly diagnosed case of alcoholism. He is not inherently a drunkard at all, has not the temperament, and would seem to be one only to the superficial judgment. He turns to drink as the result of overwork and emotional strain, and, later, in his physical revulsion to "business," he presents a very fair case of another great American disease, neuresthenia. The two vicious and unscrupulous sisters-in-law are carefully studied examples of a disease very prevalent, too, in this country, feminine vulgarity.

The Turmoil, further, is very interesting in its relation to the literature come out of Indiana. That literature up to the point of the appearance of this novel had been almost altogether that of the period when a people can't get away from boosting themselves, of a young community with a chip on its shoulder. It was a colt fearful that its end would not be held up before the world. It had not the sophistication of the time when one can laugh and "cuss" at oneself. In short, *The Turmoil* marks a point of "culture" in the march of the literature of the State.

Why is Mr. Tarkington so popular a writer? And why have some of his books, *His Own People* for one, fallen so far short of the immense popularity of others? As he sees it himself, popularity has always been an accident with him, and so has *un*popularity; both "just happened," so far, he says, as his own intentions have been concerned. He has had, there can be no doubt, the mechanical accomplishment at hand, always, to have written an unbroken series of popular books. In fact, he thinks (apparently quite honestly) that "anybody can write a popular story." For Mr. Tarkington deliberately to have set himself to produce an unbroken series of purely popular books,—nothing, one cannot fail to perceive in his talk, could have been more utterly impossible than his *doing* such a thing.

It is difficult for one to get him to put his position in so many words, as, he says, it sounds like his saying that "he is a loyal American"; but driven into a corner he will confess his faith. And to view him with justice we ought to hear it. He has never, then, "played the goat to entertain anybody." If there are "devices" here and there in his books which have an air of being bids for popular favor, devices such as the far-fetched story part of *The Flirt*, they are there not because of a crafty motive of the author's, but because he didn't know any better,—any other, better way of bringing out what he had in mind to bring out. That he put them in to please an editor or a book buyer: "Really, I'd as soon have forged a check."

"I've written things only," he declares, "as I thought they ought to be written. I thought in my youth that life could be got into books with prettier colors and more shaping than the model actually had; and I fell in with a softer, more commonplace and more popular notion of what a *story* should be.

Where that acceptance definitely stopped *in me* (though the book may not show it) was *Beauty and the Jacobin*. It was at that time that I was painting with my old ornamental picture framer. Until then, I thought they were the 'cheese,'—not for sales, but the *right* 'cheese.'" There is point, too, in noting that what now appear as very conventional features of some of Mr. Tarkington's early books, the "shaping" attempted in, for instance, *The Gentleman from Indiana*, were not so altogether conventional at the time those books were written.

As a playwright Mr. Tarkington evidently does not take matters with such intense earnestness. That is "different"; the elaborate cost of the production is to be met; the "house" to be filled; "and then I'm not a playwright anyhow." But writing books is his "work." He is writing a book now that he doesn't think anybody will read. Doesn't see why anybody wanted to read *The Turmoil*. He got to "dislike those people so much" as he wrote about them that he does not see how "anybody can stand them." He glares about the room as he tells how much he got to "hate" "those people," as if he half feared that one of them might be coming back to see him. One has an idea that if, just then, the door bell should ring, Mr. Tarkington would nervously tell the maid not to let in any of those people of *The Turmoil*.

But why *is* Mr. Tarkington so popular a writer? Because, it has repeatedly been asserted, he always has a "good story" to tell. But a study of the whole of his work certainly results in the conclusion that the "born story-teller" within him is the least of his talents, as of course it is the least valuable fellow in the heart of any artist. He doesn't care for "stories" at all, he says. Nothing, he declares, so bores him as to have someone outline a "story." However, let that go. Many people find in his books the enjoyment of a good story; and one should not quibble over what precisely a "story" is. A good story, after all, is a fabrication in which very real people seem to do very real things; and, in this sense, *Seventeen* is certainly a much better story than Wilkie Collins's *Moonstone*. At any rate, Mr. Tarkington has a brilliant gift for the art of fiction, and, having thoroughly mastered the craft of writing, he tells what he has to tell most uncommonly well. The genuine intellectual vigor which has come into his work within recent years you may take with relish, or you may let it go whistling by, according to how you are "fixed" intellectually yourself.

There is, however, a somewhat deeper explanation of the wide and general appeal which he makes. Someone (was it Mr. Howells?) has observed of Thackeray, that he was the ordinary British Philistine, plus genius. With that, as a judgment of

Thackeray, we are not, of course, at the moment concerned; nor is an implication intended that Mr. Tarkington is a regular Philistine. There is, however, this thing about him: he is very much like most people. There is nothing, except its energy, peculiar about his mind; it has no strong idiosyncratic bias, no strange, abnormal quality. At first, as in *Cherry*, he may have been excessively belletristic. That was not only not odd, but quite natural in a well educated, young writer. But, just for the joke of the thing, think, for an instant of Mr. Tarkington in connection with such a writer as, let us say, George Moore. In this wearer of the literary ermine you find laid bare a soul compacted of nearly everything that is detestable to the mind of a plain citizen going about his business in the marketplace. He has confessed consuming egotism, quivering sensibility, fastidiousness, vanity, timidity coupled with calculating shamelessness, sensuality, a streak of feline cruelty, and absolute spiritual incontinence. Or try to think of Mr. Tarkington coming along with some such perverse thinking (however shrewd) as Samuel Butler's: "the worst misfortune that can happen to any person is to lose his money; the second is to lose his health; and the loss of reputation is a bad third." Mr. Tarkington admires all those things which every decent, ordinary, simple-hearted person admires: dash, courage, honesty, honor, feminine virtue and graciousness and beauty, and so on. He hates precisely those things hated by all honest, healthy, "American" people: sham, egoism, conceit, cruelty, affectation, and so forth. In short, though he is a red hot artist (and most Americans "don't care a nickel for art"), he believes in all those things which make up the creed of the average sane, wholesome person in this country. He has infectious humor, and (though savage in attack upon what he feels to be vicious) abounding "good humor." Added to all this, he has a most winning and rich, though not at all complex, personality. He is in his own person, indeed, what most of us would like to be. In a word, doubtless his books are popular because of the same qualities that made their author popular as an undergraduate.

While Mr. Tarkington's appearance in the magazines is not confined to those of "popular" price, he does appear in these so consistently that, in the case of a writer who could go anywhere, there must be some point to this. I don't know that he has ever, since his *John-a-Dreams* days, been in a magazine addressed exclusively to the "judicious" and the "discerning," a magazine of the type which must depend for its existence upon the interest of the comparatively small class of "cultivated" readers. There is, at least, an implication in this fact that he has a relish for not appearing there. His preference, as a stage for himself, for the magazine frankly addressed to the heart of the whole lot of us is so marked that there can be little doubt that he holds it the greater triumph to be in spirit cheek by jowl with the multitude. Indeed, he has expressed some such creed in his appreciation of Riley, "the people's poet," published in *Collier's Weekly* shortly after the poet's death: "The laurel is bestowed by the people. Not even the king can make a laureate; the laurel is always bestowed by the people. Afterward the universities hear of what has happened and protect the wreath." You may hold (as I do) that it is the other way round: that it is the passionate few who make such a fuss about literature, because to them it is a thing that really matters, who create and maintain real literary reputation. However, that's not Mr. Tarkington's view.

The term "cultivated reader," and all its kin, one picks up very quickly in his presence, rubs him the wrong way. His little short of violent reaction to the whole idea of the "literary" atmosphere is a subject for, with apologies for the offensive word, the literary alienist. His friends know that at public dinners he always "winches," as he puts it, at every oratorical reference to "literature." A general aversion to anything savoring of what is popularly regarded as the literary taint is, of course, a conspicuous mark of the day of which Mr. Tarkington is so thoroughly a part. Our magazines of considerable literary traditions announce "unlitcrary" essays. But his own antipathy to the unfortunate, great popular taboo has unusual personal earmarks.

We have a bromidiom rampant among us about the author who is interested in Life rather than in literature. But we should have ample evidence in the striking range of Mr. Tarkington's literary allusion in his work, if we had no other way of knowing it, that he is sufficiently interested in literature to maintain an acquaintance, a sort of easy *camaraderie*, with the best that has been thought and done in the world.—Though these allusions, so frequent as to constitute a habit, are singularly unobtrusive, have a colloquial air, indeed, and invariably are so pat that if any of them were to be removed the omission would perceptibly weaken the woof of the exposition. In conversation, a person of pronounced literary interests would find it hard to take him on a tack where he was not at home; would, indeed, find very stimulating his alertness to all sorts of literary ideas and his active scrutiny of the claims of all sorts of literary tendencies, both past and current. He can "talk shop" to make your head spin; but it would be a considerable feat of the imagination to picture him as ever "æstheticising," in George Moore's word.

Mr. Tarkington's swarming literary opinions—or perhaps one had better say opinions of writers and on writing—strike one attempting to "size him up" as having abundant critical acuteness, and in expression are couched in phrases of a technical smack. He always "feels the ink," for instance, in the work of Alfred Noyes. There is, too, illuminating self-revelation in this observation, as, one perceives, keeping the "ink" out of it is precisely one of Mr. Tarkington's great aims in his work at present: an endeavor to present a transcript of life directly from the field, so to say, and not by way of the study. The impelling purpose of his maturity, one feels, is to be the antithesis of the editorial writer, Farwell Knowles, who was taught something of practical politics by Boss Gorgett in *In the Arena*, and to *not* "see things along book lines." Further, Mr. Howells, in his opinion, is the one genuinely American realist; Norris and Dreiser are Zola and Russian. And this pronouncement is decidedly suggestive, too, as "along of it" it occurs to one that one of the outstanding features of Mr. Tarkington's career is that he has never lurked in the purlieus of "schools," never insinuated himself into "movements."

One of the characteristic phases of our day is that many successful writers "go in for" offices in skyscrapers. The air of their modernity and practicality is further heightened by their preference for bank buildings in which to do their work. I know one who has the imperial suite, so to say, in the Harriman Bank Building; and Mr. Nicholson's "office hours" are spent in a bank building on his Washington Street. Though the principle which animates Mr. Tarkington's work certainly is distinctly incompatible with the Sir-Leslie-Stephen-*Hours-in-a-Library* kind of thing, we find him at work in an apartment which is a combination of library and art museum. The walls of the commodious, second floor, front room in the old-fashioned house in Indianapolis, which is his work-room, are lined with books to the number, certainly, of several thousand. Above the shelves the walls continue to be effaced by a swarming mass of paintings (including many portraits of himself familiar to one's memory), unusual drawings, and handsome reproductions of works, like Whistler's "Miss Alexander," familiar to any amateur of art. Down stairs the Stanford-White-Old-Curiosity-Shop effect reaches out through the dining room, and for all I know extends into the kitchen; the weird jumble being topped by a frieze of aged Italian canvases, both good and mediocre, and apparently all equally cherished by the possessor, who will dilate to the visitor over a fine thing or, with equal relish of its interest to himself, over a thing simply boring to the visitor.

Though Mr. Tarkington has got together a remarkable lot of objects of (more or less) art, he could not be called a "collector" in any strict sense of the word, that is, one who assembles works of art in accordance with some logical system. He has bought, evidently, whatever has appealed to this or that interest in him: a painting by a local painter, or a Roman fountain. And should he take a fancy to such a thing (which, one feels, is not altogether unlikely) he might, you have an idea, buy a brass monkey. Lining, or rather plastering, the hall, the paintings continue; and, with no diminishing in the effect of remarkable abundance, they mount the ascent of the stairway: Metcalf, Robert Reid, goodness knows who all are there. A sense of the fact that he has overwhelmingly cluttered up his house with riches rather than decorated it has apparently struck the owner, as he announces to the visitor that he is now building a house in Maine which will have "nothing in it, nothing at all."

The picture—not the painted one, but the real one—of Mr. Tarkington in his habit as he labors is startlingly unlike anything ever done of him in paint or print. He is collarless (the collar-button of his shirt unbuttoned), and garbed in an old and particularly evil-looking dressing-gown, which looks as if it might have been constructed of a horse-blanket which had seen active service, and had not been renovated since. This blanket accentuates the rounded stoop which he seems to take on in this chamber, a stoop so marked as to give him at moments a hunchback appearance. Removed from the handsome, and youthful, lines of his tailored clothes, with this prehistoric stoop, and in this quaint gunny-sack gown, he presents, now and then, altogether a humorously elderly effect. No, not elderly; old, very old; ancient—beyond the reckoning of years. Especially is this so when he puts on (with a trembling hand) his shell spectacles, to peer at something. And podders about the room in shuffling slippers, as he does in a kind of lean-slippered-and pantaloon manner. All in all, the visitor who has the privileged honor to penetrate into the upper fastness is likely to receive an impression of the master of the house as a *bizarre* object. Your host has the general effect of recalling to your mind some figure in a wild tale. An eccentric being, an old uncle, a miser, maybe, in a Stevenson yarn of romance. In poetic justice, a black cat should perch upon the shoulder of this figure; this ancient should keep his teeth in a glass; he should, midst squeaking wheezes and rusty cackles, poke the fire with a broken bellows.

To the imagination, in the setting here of his rich library, this picturesque gentleman might be, the last thing in the world he is, a "man of books," a bibliophile. Though a bibliophile, a man who makes of book collecting an exact science, did one scrutinize these shelves, would be very much annoyed; he would find the library as miscellaneous and democratic as the museum: the æsthete, Arthur Symons, shoulders the soldier of fortune, Richard Harding Davis. Close by one window is a sharply tilted drawing table, on the face of which rest a number of sheets of manila legal cap, the top sheet inscribed in a huge hand, "Chap. V." And on a stand by the table is a startling array of dozens and dozens of long, newly-sharpened pencils. "Sharpen 'em all the night before," explains Mr. Tarkington. Stern preparation for the coming death-grapple with that angel!

In England it is a common thing for an author to be a game-warden, a constable, or a squire, or some such thing. Mr. Tarkington is not exactly any of these things in his own "shire," but he does fill the chair of a public spirited citizen of his city. He serves on sundry committees and lends his name to the support of divers charities. A point more to our purpose here, however, is that in times of public crisis he becomes something of a publicist, and may be seen now and then hurrying along the street on his way to the newspaper office with an article in his hand to be presented for publication. This article usually is "set" in bold faced type in a "box" on the front page next day,—and makes very mediocre reading.

Now and then Mr. Tarkington has taken little

spins in the field of the essayist. He has been betrayed into an article on the manners of the Middle West, a few travel sketches, a (very "wordy") "critical introduction" to a translation of Victor Cherbuliez's *Samuel Brohl et Cie.*, at least once into a bit of "art criticism," and into other such "occasional" writings, most recently his article on drink, "Nipskillions." These, happily infrequent, performances are curiously interesting, in the same way that it is interesting and puzzling to observe that a man totally without fear in battle may be a man fearful of being left alone at night, or shrink from looking out of the top window of a skyscraper. Not only is Mr. Tarkington quite devoid of the journalist's "touch," but all inspiration appears mysteriously to desert him entirely the moment he turns from purely creative writing. And the effect, in most cases, of his "articles" mainly is to recall to the reader's mind the epigrammatic observation upon another writer that he "had no talent whatever,—only genius." It could never be said that Mr. Tarkington "disported" himself as a journalist. As a "miscellaneous writer" he is altogether too (in Mr. Herford's phrase) "intensely intense." The thing which seems to be the matter with his "journalism" is the thing which is giving him more and more force as an artist, his high seriousness. When he writes an article a monster of earnestness within him seems to rise up and take him by the throat with (to a bit confuse the figure) rather deadening effect on the reader.

What is to come we know not. But we know
That what has been was good—good to show,—

The author of *The Gentleman from Indiana* was a neophyte of rich promise. He has, after some waverings, more than amply fulfilled that early promise. He has learned his trade in all its departments. He has employed in practice as an artistic precept the moral one, to try all things and then to hold fast to that which is good. He has found his true, rare vocation, that of satirist, critic. He is in the prime of life, what is called "the very plenitude of his powers." He has entered upon a period of amazing productivity; is very much "on the job"; and appears to be "functioning" perfectly. He has gathered himself together, and set his house in order. He has been chastened by life, and success. He holds in the hollow of his hand the magic of style. He knows men (women and boys), books and cities. What sort of critical speculation may be hazarded as to what degree of excellence he may reasonably be expected yet to attain? By what he has done he has "let himself in for" a good deal to come. By what he has now written we may know that he has not yet begun to write.

Lightning Source UK Ltd.
Milton Keynes UK
UKHW020645241218
334505UK00007B/178/P